LIFE SCRIPTS

Ursula Markham is a practising hypnotherapist and stress management consultant. In addition to running her own successful clinic, she gives lectures and conducts workshops and seminars in Britain and abroad. She has appeared frequently on radio and television and is Principal of The Hypnothink Foundation which is responsible for the training of hypnotherapists and counsellors to professional level.

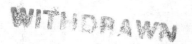

Life Scripts

HOW TO 'TALK' TO YOURSELF

FOR POSITIVE RESULTS

Ursula Markham

ELEMENT

Shaftesbury, Dorset ● Rockport, Massachusetts

Brisbane, Queensland

© Ursula Markham 1993

Published in Great Britain in 1993 by
Element Books Limited
Longmead, Shaftesbury, Dorset

Published in the USA in 1993 by
Element, Inc.
42 Broadway, Rockport, MA 01966

Published in Australia in 1993 by
Element Books Limited for
Jacaranda Wiley Limited
33 Park Road, Milton, Brisbane, 4064

Cover design by Max Fairbrother
Design by Roger Lightfoot
Typeset by Electronic Book Factory Ltd, Fife, Scotland
Printed and bound in Great Britain by
Redwood Books, Trowbridge, Wiltshire

British Library Cataloguing in Publication
data available

Library of Congress Cataloging in Publication
data available

ISBN 1–85230–432–4

Contents

To Philip and David – with my love

'No man can reveal to you aught but that which already lies half asleep in the dawning of your knowledge.'

Kahlil Gibran, *The Prophet*

Introduction

I wonder why you decided to pick up this book. There could be many different reasons – and each would be valid.

Perhaps you were intrigued by the title – *Life Scripts*. What exactly is a Life Script? How can you possibly have a script for life when there are so many aspects of it which are beyond your control? And, anyway, would they be scripts for one or would you need to join with others to make them work?

Possibly you have a problem (or even more than one) which is making you unhappy or spoiling your life in some way. Can Life Scripts really provide a method of overcoming such problems?

Could it be that you need some help in motivating yourself so that you are more able to make decisions, to work towards your goals and to fulfil that potential which you *know* lies within you. How can Life Scripts help you to achieve all this?

The answers to these and many other questions are to be found in this book. Read it, discover the value of Life Scripts for yourself – and you could be setting out on a whole new way of life.

1

About Life Scripts

We all talk to ourselves all the time. Some of us may actually speak the words aloud while others simply allow thoughts to enter our minds. Most of us use a combination of the two methods.

And how we listen to those 'internal conversations'! Whether it is the nervous person saying, 'I can't', or the champion athlete saying, 'I can', the words we repeat to ourselves play a great part in influencing our performance. This being so, surely it is possible to tailor the words we use to our own particular needs in order to help us overcome any difficulties we may be experiencing in specific areas of our lives.

In the 1920s Emile Coué ran a clinic in Nancy, France where he taught his patients what he called 'Induced Autosuggestion'. This was a form of self-help which required them to repeat particular phrases to themselves over a period of time. These phrases were designed to help overcome any negative beliefs which had become fixed in the patient's subconscious. Although Coué was responsible for helping many who suffered from distressing physical and emotional conditions, the saying for which he is best known in Britain is one which became fashionable in society after his visit in November, 1921. For some time afterwards the fashionable ladies and gentlemen of the day could be heard murmuring to themselves, 'Every day and in every way I'm getting better and better'. And some of them *did* find their lives improving in the way they wished. Unfortunately, however, many of those who repeated that phrase did so because it was the 'in' thing to do rather than stopping to think about what they were saying and doing.

Life Scripts are designed to be spoken, but also to be thought about. They are a way of making use of all the talking to ourselves that we do anyway. When a patient consults a hypnotherapist much of what takes place is talking. The hypnosis which is involved serves to help the subconscious absorb what is being said. The altered state of hypnosis itself lies somewhere between a deep relaxation and a light meditation and is a vital first stage if the spoken words are to have any real effect. If you want Life Scripts to work well for you, you too will have to learn how to relax deeply – indeed the first script you will be given will be for a deep relaxation technique.

Everyone has something about themselves they would like to change. It might be a simple but upsetting habit – such as nail biting – or it might be learning to come to terms with a tangle of emotions brought about by distressing events from the past. Whatever it is that you would like to change, Life Scripts can help you.

WHY LIFE SCRIPTS?

It has been found that, on average, we take in:

- 20 per cent of what we read
- 30 per cent of what we hear
- 40 per cent of what we see
- 50 per cent of what we say
- 60 per cent of what we do
  but
- *90 per cent of what we see, hear, say and do.*

Life Scripts will give you the opportunity to absorb and work on that 90 per cent.

Life Scripts are just what they sound like – a series of

scripts designed to help you improve your life, whatever problems you may encounter now or at any time in the future. You can have these scripts read to you by another person or you can read them yourself, recording them on cassette so that they are ready to play back whenever it is convenient for you to do so. They also contain all the ingredients for that 90 per cent absorption mentioned earlier.

Seeing: You will see the printed words as you read them aloud;

Saying: You will speak the words as you record them on to the cassette;

Hearing: You will hear those words when the cassette is played back;

Doing: You will turn those words into images in your mind as you practise the technique of visualization while listening to the cassette.

Visualization

The ability to visualize – to see pictures in your mind – is an important aspect of working with Life Scripts. You will need to translate the spoken words into images if you are to convince your subconscious of the inevitability of your success. Think of it as a form of 'mental rehearsal'. If you were to take part in a play you would rehearse not only your words but your actions so that, on opening night, everything would go splendidly. In just the same way, if you are to overcome your problems you need to be able to visualize yourself acting as though the words being spoken were already fact.

It is not as hard as you might think. Although as we grow up and become involved in the practicalities of life, many of us get out of the habit of visualizing, it is an ability we all possess. In fact, the only people who are not able to visualize at all are those who were born blind – the rest of us just need a little practice.

If you think you are not adept at creating visual images in your mind, just consider all the things you learned as a child – long before you were able to speak. You learned to recognize those who were important to you; you knew what a toy was for; you knew what to do when given a drink or a biscuit. And yet no words were available to you. You knew all these things because you had seen them before and had retained the images in your mind.

Many people are very good at negative visualization; they can see themselves failing at something and can remember the disasters of their lives. However, it is the positive imagery they need to work at. But it is that positive imagery, combined with the seeing, hearing and saying, which will enable them to change themselves in whatever way they wish.

Suppose you are one of those who doubts his (or her) own ability to create visual images – what can you do to improve? Try thinking of the imagination as a muscle. Like any muscle of the body, if you don't exercise it, it will become weak and flabby. And, like any muscle of the body, you cannot just exercise it once and find it firm and strong again; you need to flex it daily, building strength and power little by little. Try following the three steps below, allowing yourself about a week to practise each one before going on to the next.

Step 1

Look at the list of words which follows. Read them aloud to yourself, one at a time. As you read each one, stop and try to create the object in your imagination. Don't worry if you find this difficult at first or if the image is vague or short-lived. Persevere and you will find it easier every day.
– house
– tree
– tomato
– cow
– baby

– sea
– chair
– daffodil
– telephone
– teapot.

Step 2

Once you have mastered the first step, stretch your imagination by giving it scenes to visualize. These should be scenes you know well – some examples are given below but you can choose anything which appeals to you.
– your bedroom when a child
– the interior of any of the rooms in your present home
– a place where you have spent a pleasant holiday.

Step 3

Now you need to incorporate some action into your imagined scenes so that you become accustomed to visualizing yourself *doing* something. It is important at this point to avoid anything which you would find difficult or distressing in reality so try to keep to simple, pleasant activities. A few examples are given here but, once again, you can substitute whatever activity you prefer.
– walk along a familiar route, noticing the scenery around you
– climb a flight of stairs
– prepare some food
– indulge in a favourite hobby or pastime.

The benefits of recording your own Life Scripts

• It is quite possible to have someone else read the words to you from the book but by doing so you will lose the 'saying' element which is necessary if you are to achieve that 90 per cent intake.

- You will be able to insert any words which make the script more personal for you. Those printed must, of necessity, be written in general terms but you can include any relevant names (your own or other people's) to give the script more validity and power. In addition, you can also insert any references which are of particular relevance to your own situation. For example, if you have a fear of flying and know that you need to take a flight to Paris next June, you can incorporate that fact into the script at the appropriate point. The more personal you can make your script, the more effective it will be.

- You can make several attempts at recording each script, continuing until you are completely happy with the result. You might find that you like to have soothing music playing in the background; if so, you will need to experiment with the type of music and its volume.

- You can choose your best time of day for using the cassette you have made rather than having to rely on the availability of someone else's. You need a time when you can sit quietly and comfortably, certain that you will not be disturbed and that you do not have to rush off to a pressing appointment.

- You can work at your own pace – and this will vary, not only from person to person but from stage to stage. There are no hard and fast rules. What takes one person six days might take another ten. All that matters is that you are completely satisfied with the results obtained from one script before proceeding to the next.

USES OF LIFE SCRIPTS

This book contains scripts for most of the problems which you are likely to encounter. However, should you feel that yours is slightly different, you will learn how to adapt the scripts given to suit your own situation. The categories of problems covered include:

- Habits

– smoking
– overeating
– nail biting

- Fears and phobias

– agoraphobia
– claustrophobia
– fear of insects

(Obviously, it will not be possible to cover all of the many phobias, but clear instructions will be given for converting the scripts to suit your own particular problem.)

- Dealing with difficult emotions

– bereavement
– break-up of a relationship
– guilt
– fear

(This section will also include a technique for retaining positive emotions and committing them to your subconscious memory so that they can be recalled at will.)

- Health

– dealing with pain (and the care that should be taken when doing so)
– before and after surgery
– panic attacks
– asthma
– migraine
– insomnia
– pre-menstrual tension

- Fulfilling potential

– developing creativity
– learning and memory
– sport
– exams, tests, interviews

- During and after pregnancy

– communicating with your unborn child
– preparing for childbirth
– after the birth

- Loving yourself

– removing negative influences
– negating past programming
– the results of abuse
– learning to love yourself
– attuning to the natural world
– enhancing relationships

- Preparing for the future

– goal-setting (short- and long-term)
– motivation
– creating your own Life Scripts for your future.

RELAXATION

We have already seen that the ability to relax is one of the essential requirements if you are to obtain maximum benefit from your Life Scripts. Life has become so hectic and stressful in recent years that relaxation has become, for many, a forgotten art. The schoolchild being urged by anxious parents, peers or teachers to perform well; the woman trying to deal with the responsibilities of family and career; the couple working hard to build a home and hoping that jobs are safe in such uncertain times; the older man realizing that some old ambitions may now never be achieved and wrestling with fears of growing old; the elderly person trying to manage on a pension which seems to buy less each year – these are just a few of the people experiencing the extreme pressures of current life. For each of them, as for many others, learning to relax might not solve all their practical problems but it could certainly prevent them being added to by a breakdown in mental or physical well-being.

Yet relaxation is a skill which can be learned at any

time. Once you know the words and actions, all it takes is practice. And, for anyone who wishes to bring about deliberate improvements in their life, it is an important first step. It is only in the relaxed state that the words you are going to say to yourself can really penetrate not only the conscious but the subconscious mind.

So the first script is one designed to help you re-learn how to relax. There are several essential stages to this:

- Release of muscular tension. To relax any muscle, you first need to tense it as much as possible – but do note that, should you have physical pain in any area of your body, you should not actually increase the tension of that particular part but simply focus your attention on it.

- Establishment of a regular breathing pattern. The majority of us do not breathe correctly most of the time. Our breathing tends to be shallow, coming from the chest area rather than from the diaphragm. This section of the script will ask you to concentrate upon your breathing so that you can establish a slow and regular rhythm.

- Creation of a pleasant image. There are various reasons for this. If your relaxation script were merely to ask you to clear your mind of all thought, you would find it extremely difficult. In fact, if you were not given something specific to think about, all those niggling little problems surrounding you would probably force their way in – and you would end up being anything but relaxed! By creating an enjoyable picture in your mind you not only keep out negative thought but you come to associate relaxation (and therefore your Life Script) with something pleasant, calming and positive.

  There is no one image which will be the best for everyone. While one person may enjoy a visualization which includes a lake or sea, it will not be very relaxing for the individual who happens to have a phobia about water. The person who knows that he suffers from hayfever may experience discomfort if he successfully visualizes a cornfield. So you will find that, when it comes to the place in the script where you have to describe the image, you will be given several from which to choose. (Of course, you may prefer to use another one entirely; provided it is something you find pleasant and peaceful, go ahead.)

Read through the script first so that you are familiar with it and can decide which image would best suit you. Then record it on cassette, with or without background music.

Relaxation script

As I sit here in my comfortable chair in a quiet room, I close my eyes.

I tense the muscles in my feet as tightly as I can before letting them become limp again. Now I do the same to my legs and thighs – tense them and then relax them. I clench my fists and cause the muscles in my arms to become rigid . . . and now I relax them, allowing my hands to lie loosely in my lap. Next I concentrate on the trunk of my body, feeling the muscles tense and then letting them go so that my body becomes heavy in the chair. Now it is time to focus on the area where tension is usually most noticeable – my neck, shoulders, jaw and face. I tighten my shoulder muscles and those in my neck; I clench my jaw and frown as hard as I can. Now I allow all those muscles to relax; my shoulders drop, my jaw becomes slack and all the tension leaves my forehead.

Now I am going to spend a few moments concentrating on the rhythm of my breathing and ensuring that I breathe from the diaphragm rather than simply from the upper chest. I breathe slowly in . . . and out; in . . . and out; in . . . and out; in . . . and out; and in . . . and out.

Next I am going to use my imagination to deepen that sense of relaxation. I imagine my feet growing heavier and heavier – as though they had turned to stone. Still using my powers of imagination, I feel that heaviness creeping slowly past my ankles, up my legs, past my knees and up my thighs until it reaches my hips. In just the same way I imagine my hands becoming heavier and then feel that sensation spreading past my wrists, up my forearms, past my elbows and up my upper arms until it reaches my shoulders.

Now I concentrate on the whole of my body and I become aware of its weight as I relax in my comfortable chair. The heavy feeling spreads upwards from my lower body, past my waist to my chest area; now it travels to my shoulders and then up to my neck. Finally I am aware that my head is comfortable and relaxed, my jaw is loose and my eyelids feel heavy.

Now that my body is in a state of relaxation, I am going to spend some time contemplating the image I have chosen.

(*At this stage continue with whichever of the following images you prefer.*)

1. I am walking along a beautiful deserted beach. The sand is white under a deep blue, cloudless sky. The air is pure and clean and there is a gentle breeze blowing.

I am aware of many sensations – of the feeling of the warm sand beneath my bare feet, the sun caressing my face, my arms and my back, the breeze touching my hair. The deep blue of the sky is reflected in the sea below and I watch the gentle wavelets as they play on the shore. I can smell the clean, fresh air just tinged with the aroma of the sea. This is a wonderful, beautiful and peaceful place.

The white sand stretches as far as the eye can see. Here and there on the beach are small clusters of palm trees providing shade. I approach one of these groups of trees and discover a soft, pink fluffy towel spread on the sand beneath them – just waiting for me to lie down on it.

I stretch out on my back on that soft towel and close my eyes. I am aware of the warmth of the sand beneath the towel – a warmth which I can feel on my back and on the back of my legs. It causes all the tension to leave my body as I relax more and more. The leaves of the tall palm trees shade me from the heat of the sun but the air is still warm and I can hear the leaves rustling quietly as the gentle breeze blows.

My entire mind and body relax as I absorb the warmth from the atmosphere and I lie there peacefully, listening to the sound of the tiny waves breaking on the shore and the occasional distant seabird calling. I will stay here on this beautiful beach and relax for several minutes until I feel I want to return.

2. I am standing in a country lane which winds and twists ahead of me. Around me I can see fields and hedgerows and in the distance are the gentle slopes of soft, blue-grey hills. It is a warm spring day; there are blossoms on the trees and bushes and leaves and shoots are a fresh, new green. Small white clouds hover in the blue sky and the spring sunshine gives a sparkle to the scene.

I begin to walk along that lane, looking to the right and the left, aware of how beautiful and peaceful it is. I can feel the sun on my skin; I can smell the green newness of the plants around me. Birds are singing in the trees and the air is filled with natural sounds – the rustle of leaves in the breeze, the distant lowing of a cow in a field.

After I have walked a short distance I find myself at the edge of a small wood where the trees are straight and strong and very, very old. I put out my hand and touch one of those ancient trees and I feel the warm roughness of the bark. I am aware of the energy within that tree.

I walk on into the wood where it is a little cooler and a little darker because the leaves of the trees meet far above my head. Ahead of me I can see a single patch of sunlight – a place where the leaves of the trees do not meet. Going forwards, I step into that patch of sunlight and am aware of the rays of the spring sun washing over me like a warm, friendly shower – washing away all the stress and tension I have accumulated in my mind and my body. I stretch my arms up to the sun, allowing those warm, relaxing rays to touch every part of me.

And now I lower my arms and, still in the sunlight, lean against one of those old trees. I shall stay here for a few minutes to allow the sense of relaxation to spread through me.

3. I open a big heavy door and find myself entering a warm, comfortable room. This room is decorated in my favourite colours and the furniture in it is old and comfortable. Set in one wall is a large window and the view from that window is the one I would most like to see.

As I look around the room I can see a big fireplace with a log fire burning there. In front of the fire is a large, comfortable-looking chair. The room is filled with the things that I like – books, pictures, ornaments. Vases of flowers scent the air and delight the eye.

I walk around the room, looking at the pictures, bending to smell the flowers, running my hand along the old wood of the furniture.

When I come to the big armchair in front of the fire, I decide to sit in it for a while. The chair supports and suits my body as though it had been designed just for me. It is firm but comfortable and its back is high enough to support my head and neck. I lie back in that chair and relax.

I can feel the warmth from the fire on my legs and I am aware that my whole body is relaxing. I look around and realize that this room is mine alone. No one else has ever entered it – and no one but me will ever do so. There is a tranquillity here which makes it a very special place.

I can hear the logs crackling as they burn in the grate and I turn my head to watch the flames dancing in the fire. The glow from the fire, the movement of the flames and the feeling of peace combine to relax my body and my mind. I close my eyes and decide to spend a few minutes relaxing in that comfortable chair in my very special room.

(*Whichever image you have chosen, continue now as follows.*)

Now that I am completely relaxed, I know that my conscious and subconscious minds are in the best possible state to absorb those thoughts which are going to help me change and improve my life in the way I have chosen.

I would suggest that you record this relaxation technique on a long cassette – say, forty-five minutes per side. This will enable you to continue on the same side of the same tape with the appropriate Life Script and would enable you to listen to the latter without necessitating a break which might disturb your sense of relaxation.

AFFIRMATIONS

Affirmations are positive phrases which you repeat over and over again to yourself and, while I do not believe that they are sufficient in themselves to bring about the necessary changes, I do feel that they can be a very valuable aid during the self-help process. Because they can be of assistance, you will find after each Life Script some affirmations you might like to use to reinforce the work you are already doing.

These affirmations can be used in various ways:

- You can speak them aloud to yourself as you go about your daily tasks – mowing the lawn, brushing your hair, even doing the washing up! You do not actually have to concentrate too hard on the meaning of the words of the affirmations – the fact that you are repeating them frequently will be sufficient for them to have an effect.

- You can record them on a separate cassette and let

them play over and over while you do other things. Once again, you do not have to listen actively to them – you will still hear them on a subconscious level.

- You can write each affirmation on a separate piece of card and keep these cards with you to be looked at and read at frequent intervals during the day. It will only take a few moments at any one time but will go a long way towards reinforcing the message of the Life Script on which you are working.

- You can write them on 'Post-it' notes. Because they leave no mark when they are taken down, you can stick the affirmations all over the place – on your bathroom mirror, your kitchen cupboard, your front door or your office desk. Just as it is not necessary to concentrate on the words you speak, you do not have to stop and deliberately read the words written – your subconscious mind will read and absorb the messages without you even having to think about it.

Now it is time for you to begin to help yourself. Think about your life and the area where you would most like to make changes and turn to the Life Scripts designed to help you along that path.

2

Habit-breaking

Habits can range from the slightly irritating to the positively life-threatening. If you whistle through your teeth or constantly drum your fingers on the table, you might risk having something thrown at you but you are unlikely to damage your health permanently. Smoking, however, is another matter altogether. Not only do you risk your own health but that of others too. More and more evidence is coming to light about the real danger to health of passive smoking, particularly among the very young and the very old.

SMOKING

The first habit we are going to deal with in this chapter is that of smoking. The smoker has to overcome three things if he wishes to give up. (I am not being sexist by referring to 'he'; it is simply less clumsy than repeating 'he or she', 'him or her' each time. So, unless completely inappropriate, please take 'he' as referring to either sex.)

The desire to smoke

This is perhaps the easiest problem to overcome and is therefore the first one tackled. Whatever the method someone tries to use to give up smoking, none will work on a permanent basis without the honest desire to quit. And there is all the difference in the world between *wanting* to stop smoking and thinking that you should. There is an even greater difference between wanting to stop and *someone else* thinking you should – whether that someone is your doctor, your employer or a member of your family.

Because it is so important that you truly want to stop smoking, you need to think about your reasons before even setting about trying to do so. Those reasons will obviously vary greatly between individuals. One person may be worried about the money he is spending while another feels that smoking is increasingly coming to be seen as antisocial and does not wish to cause offence. The parent may wish to have a smoke-free home for his child to grow up in while the employee, compelled to work in a smoke-free office, may not wish to lose his job.

When you come to use the first in the series of scripts, you will find several passages in brackets. These refer to some of the many reasons for giving up smoking. Naturally they will not all apply to you so you will need to decide which of them you wish to include.

The habit

The majority of people, especially if they have been smoking for many years, are not even aware of the majority of cigarettes (or cigars) they have during the day. They certainly do not actively enjoy them all. As a hypnotherapist, I have been consulted over many years by hundreds of people who wish to stop smoking. Whether they normally smoke ten, twenty, thirty or even more in a day, when asked to list those they really enjoy, the number is seldom more than four or five. Some people particularly like the first one in the morning or the last one at night. Some enjoy the one they have after a meal. I have known people say that a cigarette at work is enjoyable because it calms them down when they feel under pressure – yet others insist that they only relish those they have in a social situation.

Perhaps if all smokers were able to have only those cigarettes they really enjoyed they would be able to keep the situation under control. The trouble is that they smoke all the others too – often without tasting them, without thinking about them, without particularly liking them. You know the sort of scenario I am thinking about – the telephone rings so out come the cigarettes; you're in a pub with friends and someone hands you an open packet and, before you even think what you are doing, you have taken one and smoked it without ever considering whether you wanted it or not.

The second script deals with the habit side of smoking by making you very aware of every cigarette you take, what it tastes like and how you feel about it.

Addiction

Of course a major factor of the habit of smoking is the actual addiction to nicotine. This is the aspect which takes the longest to overcome, but it is quite possible to do so. By the time you have completed the three Life Scripts designed to help you stop smoking, the addiction will already be diminishing. It is to facilitate this that the giving up is done in stages rather than all at once.

Although the Life Script technique given has been tried and tested and found to work extremely well with smokers, it is not sufficient for dealing with addiction to alcohol or to hard drugs. For either of these, it is essential to seek outside professional help – although you may find some of the later Life Scripts useful when it comes to understanding why your dependency arose in the first place and overcoming any emotional negativity which contributed to it.

Life Scripts

Smoking script – 1

Now that I am relaxed and comfortable, I am going to spend some time thinking about the habit of smoking and what I feel about it.

Because I know that it will be impossible for me permanently to give up smoking unless the desire to do so is deep within me, I am going to use this time to consider what I feel about cigarettes (cigars/tobacco) and why I am contemplating giving them up.

(I like to think that I am in control of as much of my life as possible and I do not enjoy the feeling that smoking has taken such a hold of me that I am unable to resist. I do not really want to think that I am the puppet of the tobacco industry. I realize that all those tales of smoking calming the nerves, making people appear smart or sophisticated and preventing them from overeating are nothing but stories invented by the advertisers employed by that industry and I am not prepared to be gullible or to fool myself about the reality of the situation. I – and only I – shall decide whether or not I wish to smoke in the future.)

(With each day that passes I become more and more aware of the smell of stale tobacco on other people – on their clothes, their skin, their hair and their breath. I do not want others to find the smell of my clothes, skin, hair or breath offensive.)

(I want to live as long and as healthy a life as possible. While there may be aspects of my health about which I can do little, here is an area where I am in charge – where the decisions I make can have a very real effect upon my health in the future. I choose not to put myself deliberately in a position where I am likely to end up finding it difficult to breathe or where I am in constant pain.)

(I love my family and I do not want to harm them in any way. I would like my children to grow up in a tobacco-free environment. I don't wish to harm them, either by forcing them to become passive smokers or by setting an example which they may later follow. I know that the children of smokers are more likely to become smokers themselves and, even if I manage to avoid any tobacco-induced deterioration in my own health, I do not wish to be responsible for the future failure in health of my children.)

(As an expectant mother it is up to me to give the child I am carrying as good a start in life as possible. I realize that, should I continue to smoke, my baby is likely to be born smaller and with less resistance to infection than would be the case if I were to give up.)

(The cost of tobacco is constantly rising and I know that there are far more important and enjoyable things I could do with the money.)

(I am no longer allowed to smoke in the place where I work. I do not wish to lose my job by trying to do so nor do I want to keep interrupting my work by having to leave the premises in order to feed my addiction.)

I have thought deeply about my reasons for wanting to stop smoking and have come to the decision that I shall give up for good. I shall do so because *I* wish it and not because I am being cajoled or compelled by anyone else. I may stop today if I wish; I may cut down the amount I smoke or I may decide upon a date in the near future and make a commitment with myself that I shall stop smoking on that day.

Work with this script until you feel convinced in your own mind that you really want to stop smoking. It may take a couple of days or it may take a week – there is no right or wrong amount of time. Even if you decide that you are not ready to give up smoking yet, you will probably find that the serious thought you have given to the matter will be enough to reduce considerably the number of cigarettes you want.

Suggested affirmations

- I have a will of my own and I choose not to smoke
- I want to live as long and healthy a life as possible
- I wish to protect those I love from the effects of smoking.

Smoking script – 2

I have made the decision that I no longer wish to smoke so, even though I may not decide yet to stop completely, I shall certainly reduce the number of cigarettes I have.

From this moment on, I shall be aware of every cigarette I have. I shall no longer be someone compelled by habit to smoke. I shall only do so if I truly *want* to and only if I enjoy the taste and sensation of what I am smoking.

I imagine myself in a situation where I am offered a cigarette and I take one, without being aware of what I am doing. I place it between my lips and someone lights it for me. Suddenly my mouth is filled with the worst taste imaginable – something which is made up of all those flavours I most detest. I am aware of this foul taste filling my mouth and my throat and I can imagine the poisoned blackness of the nicotine spreading to my throat and chest, making my eyes water. ... Now that taste and that sensation have gone and I can breathe cool, clean, fresh air again.

If at any time in the future I should happen to take a cigarette without thinking what I am doing, the first puff of it will be enough to recreate that evil taste and terrible sensation. This will be sufficient to make me become fully aware and, because I am the one who has chosen not to smoke, I shall put the cigarette out immediately.

If I have made a deliberate decision to smoke

a particular cigarette, I shall be aware of all the sensations which accompany it and will be able to consider whether or not they are pleasurable. Do I really like the taste – and, if I have just eaten a good meal, do I want to ruin the flavours by filling my mouth with tobacco smoke? Am I screwing up my eyes, causing my skin to look old? Is the smoke rising, making my clothes and my hair smell of stale tobacco? Is that cigarette really worth it?

I imagine what a delight it would be never again to be dependent upon smoking and to know that, at last, I am in control of my own life.

Work with this script until you reach a stage where you are only smoking a very few cigarettes. Then go on to the final one.

Suggested affirmations

- I shall be fully aware of each cigarette I smoke
- If I take a cigarette without thinking, its foul taste will make me aware of what I am doing
- I will feel happy and successful each time I consider having a cigarette and choose not to.

Smoking script – 3

I am now smoking very little and I have reached the point where I am going to choose whether or not to continue.

Because I have reduced my tobacco intake so much, my addiction to nicotine has also been reduced and therefore I shall suffer no ill effects by cutting out these last few cigarettes. As I become a non-smoker, my self-esteem increases – I have every right to feel proud of myself for achieving something so worthwhile. I have reduced the risk to my own health and to that of other people.

As I sit here, comfortable and relaxed, I imagine a busy motorway on a very hot summer's day. The heat is so great that the surface of the road becomes soft and sticky. Now I visualize that same road on a cool day – the surface is hard enough for cars and lorries to drive on without leaving a single mark. I am aware that the surface of that motorway is covered with tar – the same substance contained in the cigarettes I used to smoke. When inhaled it is soft and warm but as it cools it becomes rock-hard – hard enough to clog up arteries and air passages completely, leaving them unable to function. I want my body to function well and so I choose not to damage it by allowing tar to harden within it.

A wonderful feeling of success and achievement comes over me as I realize that, because I have made my own choices, I am now a non-smoker.

Suggested affirmations

- I am a non-smoker
- I have succeeded
- I am in control of my life.

CONTROLLING OVEREATING

I have deliberately used this heading as opposed to talking about 'weight loss' because some eating disorders are caused by deep emotional or psychological problems. Eating disorders of this sort require professional assistance and will only show superficial reaction to Life Scripts. The majority of overweight adults, however, simply eat too much. And, of course, 'too much' varies from person to person according to their personal metabolism and to their lifestyle.

There are two Life Scripts for controlling overeating. For many people the first one will be all they need to use until they reach their desired weight. The second one should be used if, even though eating has been reduced, a plateau has been reached and no weight reduction is noted.

You will see that at no time is a particular diet specified. That is because, using this method, you have no need to follow a specific diet. You are going to learn to listen to your body and understand its needs. If you were allowed 1000 calories a day and by nine o'clock at night you had only consumed 800, you would probably raid the kitchen to see what you could have to supply that other 200. But perhaps on that day you only need 800 calories – whereas on the next day you might need 1200.

In addition, there is no such thing as a forbidden food. If you were to be told that you could eat anything in the world except cheesecake, the first time you felt a bit bored or depressed the one thing you would crave would be cheesecake. Also, as soon as you reached your desired weight, you would rush to taste all those things which had not been allowed – probably with disastrous results.

One thing I would suggest; never weigh yourself more than once a week. The daily fluctuation in water in the body can vary (particularly in women) and you might therefore get a faulty reading – which would either result in false elation or false despondency. Keep to once a week and you will be able to see whether you are losing weight or not.

Overeating script – 1

I am feeling very relaxed and comfortable and I have made a calm decision that I would like to do something to change my eating habits. I realize that the only way these habits can be permanently altered is gradually so I am not going to attempt crash diets or those which require me to cut out certain types of food altogether.

I know that most people eat to excess either because it has become a habit or because they tend to eat according to the time on the clock rather than because they are hungry. I am going to learn to listen to my body and follow its needs rather than be a slave to time or habit.

As I sit here relaxing, I imagine that I have just finished eating a good and satisfying meal – perhaps a Sunday lunch, perhaps a Christmas dinner. That meal has left me feeling pleasantly full, but not uncomfortably so. I remember that feeling of having enjoyed a meal and being so satisfied that no other food would tempt me. Because I intend to learn to become aware of my body and its needs, that satisfied feeling will remain with me for most of the time. The only time it will disappear and leave me feeling hungry is when I actually need food for my health's sake.

There are only two simple rules to be followed if I wish to change my eating habits. The first is that, if I feel hungry, I *must* eat. There is no virtue in allowing that hunger to become painful as I would then be unlikely to eat sensibly. And when I do eat, I can eat anything I wish – provided I am hungry and provided I stop when I stop feeling hungry. If I am to learn to listen to my body, I shall begin by having a smaller portion of food than previously. Once I have eaten that, I shall stop and ask myself whether I am still hungry. If I am, I shall eat some more but, if I am not, I won't eat anything else at all. I do not have to be deprived of food I enjoy; I simply have to save it until later when I am hungry again.

The second rule is that, if I am not hungry, I *must not eat anything at all*. It does not matter what time it is or what time I usually eat – if I am not hungry, I shall not do so. If I want to be sociable with others, I can still sit at the table with them and, because liquids are not limited, I can have a cold or hot drink. I can still have my meal – but at a later time when I feel hungry.

As I sit here relaxing, I visualize myself being the

shape and size I intend to become. I see myself
wearing an outfit which only looks good on someone
of that shape and size. I see myself from every angle
– front, back, side – looking wonderful in the clothes
I have imagined. Nothing is pulling, stretching or
gaping: it all fits perfectly and I look marvellous. This
is the way I shall look when I have changed my eating
habits and lost any excess weight.

Suggested affirmations

- I am learning to listen to my body and to know whether
  or not I am hungry
- If I am not hungry, I choose not to eat
- I can picture myself a slim and attractive person, in
  clothes I would truly like to wear.

The following script should be used if you find your
weight loss is slowing down even though you have learned
to determine whether or not you are hungry.

Overeating script – 2

I am feeling really pleased with myself because I have
learned to listen to my body's needs and thereby
change my eating habits and lose some weight.

If my weight loss has slowed down, I realize that
this is because my metabolism is adjusting to my
new eating pattern and not because I am doing
anything wrong.

To counteract the slowing down of my weight loss,
I am going to use the most powerful tool I possess –
my own imagination.

As I relax, I visualize myself standing next to an
enormous glass of fresh drinking-water. The glass is
so large that it is almost as tall as I am. There is a

straw in the glass; I place the end of the straw in my mouth and begin to drink the water. I drink and drink until all the water has gone; this has the effect of making me feel very full and not interested in eating at the moment.

Next time I think I am hungry, before having anything to eat, I shall pour myself a normal-sized glass of water and drink all of it. Then I will stop and ask myself whether I am still hungry. If I am, I shall go ahead and eat but, if I am not, I shall wait until later when my hunger returns.

Once again I imagine myself as being the shape and size I intend to become, wearing those clothes which will look so good on me when I have reached my target. Because of the weight I have already lost and the changes I have already made in my eating habits, I know that the picture in my imagination is much nearer to becoming reality and that, with every day that passes, I come closer and closer to achieving it.

I am also aware that, because I have changed my pattern of eating in this gradual way and because I have chosen to do so, that change is permanent and I shall neither go back to old habits nor put on weight again once my target has been reached.

Suggested affirmations

- A glass of water will make me feel full
- I am getting nearer and nearer to my desired shape and size
- I am changing my eating pattern for ever.

NAIL BITING

I have chosen this as the sample 'irritating habit' because it is one for which I am so frequently consulted. But, with a little adaptation, you can use the ideas put forward in these scripts to put an end to any other habit you may have. Remember that it will only work if the desire to stop whatever you are doing is *yours*. The fact that someone else does not like what you do will not provide sufficient motivation.

There are many reasons why someone might want to stop biting their nails:

• It makes hands look unsightly
• In some cases it can be quite painful, causing soreness and bleeding
• No one likes to think they are doing something because they simply cannot help themselves
• It is embarrassing to be caught doing it.

As with other habits, nail biting is often done quite unconsciously so the first stage is to make you aware each time you do it. Sometimes this is enough in itself to make you stop – particularly if you are worried about the appearance of your hands.

If lack of awareness is not the only problem, it is often helpful to give yourself permission to bite *one nail* – whichever one you choose. In this way you are not being deprived of your habit all at once but you are giving the other nine nails a chance to strengthen and grow. Once this has happened, the final stage is to give up biting that one last fingernail. This is usually the easiest step as you will by then be anxious to have all your nails looking and feeling good.

Nail biting script – 1

I have decided that I want to stop biting my nails. This is my wish and so I shall be able to fulfil it. I have thought about my reasons for wanting to stop. They are that:

(I am ashamed of the way my hands look to myself and to other people.)

(It causes me pain and my fingertips are often sore, with torn skin.)

(I do not want my children to see me and copy my habit.)

(I wish to take charge of my life and not to be a slave to any habit.)

(I feel really embarrassed when I see other people looking at my hands or when they catch me actually biting my nails.)

I know that nail biting is a habit and that I am often unaware of the fact that I am doing it. I intend to become fully aware in the future. Because I have *chosen* not to bite my nails any more, that awareness will be sufficient to bring to my notice what I am doing and to make me stop.

As I relax, I imagine that I have before me a jar of colourless, odourless liquid and a small paintbrush. That liquid has an evil taste which lasts for a long time. I visualize myself carefully painting each nail in turn with the colourless liquid, knowing that the horrible taste is being transferred to the nail itself.

If, at any time in the future, I happen to put my fingers to my mouth in order to bite my nails, I shall immediately become aware of that terrible taste and I will pull my fingers away from my mouth at once. By using this method I shall ensure that I am always made conscious of what I am doing and so can make a choice as to whether I continue or not.

And now, still relaxing comfortably, I imagine my hands as they will be when my nails have grown again. I see myself using my hands in the way I normally do and, as I watch, I feel proud of the shape and strength of my finger nails.

Suggested affirmations

- I shall always be conscious of the fact that my fingers are near my mouth

- I choose to stop biting my nails
- My hands and nails will soon look very good.

Nail biting script – 2

By using the power of my mind, I have helped myself to become aware each time I put my fingers to my mouth to bite my nails.

I have chosen not to bite them any more but, until the habit is completely broken, I give myself permission to bite one nail on one hand. Because I am now in control of the situation, I shall only bite that one nail and no other.

In the meantime, all my other nails will grow longer and stronger until they look just as I would wish them to. Once again I recreate in my mind the image of my hands when all ten nails have grown to be the shape I would really like. I imagine how it would feel to be really proud of my hands and nails and to be happy for anyone to see them at any time.

Suggested affirmations

- I am proud of the progress I have made
- I permit myself to bite the one fingernail I have selected
- I visualize my hands looking just as I would like them to.

Nail biting script – 3

I am very proud of what I have achieved. I have managed to overcome a habit which has been with me for years. I have done it because I made a deliberate decision to do so and therefore I know that, provided I choose to do something and I work towards it, I can achieve whatever I wish.

My hands and nails are now looking almost perfect. All I have to do is to stop biting that one final fingernail. This will be very easy to do as I have broken the chains of unconscious behaviour and of habit.

As I relax, feeling warm and comfortable, I visualize my hands being stretched out in front of me and see that all the nails on both of them now look perfect. They are strong and well-shaped and the skin around them has healed. I am proud of the way they look and happy for anyone to see them at any time.

I realize that, having broken the habit, it has gone for ever and will never return. I am in control of this area of my life.

Suggested affirmations

- I do not bite any of my nails
- I shall never bite my nails again
- Breaking this habit has increased my self-esteem and my awareness of the fact that I can control many areas of my life.

You will realize that breaking any habit does more than reduce your risk of tobacco-related illness, help you lose weight or give you hands to be proud of. By overcoming something over which you formerly felt you had no control, you improve your self-image and your belief in yourself as a person who is in control of more areas of his life than previously. This in turn will help you to become a more assertive person and to deal with any problems which may arise in the future.

3

Phobias

In this chapter we are going to be looking at the problems caused by phobias – illogical fears – as opposed to fears which have a logical basis (and which will be dealt with later).

No phobia arises spontaneously, even though at times it may appear that this is so. There is always a reason for it, but problems arise when efforts are made to discover that cause as this can prove very difficult. After all, if the initial fear was great enough to cause a phobia which may last and increase over a period of several years, it is certainly great enough for you to have done all you can to block it from your memory.

It is possible, by means of hypnosis, to take someone back to an earlier period in their life to unearth the underlying cause of their phobia but this can prove quite a laborious task – particularly if the patient himself has no idea when or how it began – and a certain amount of trial and error may be necessary. In my own practice, I tend to do whatever the patient wants. If he feels it is essential to find the root cause, I am willing to help him do so, however long it may take. However, I do point out to him that such discovery actually makes no difference to the treatment which follows for overcoming the phobia.

If you are an adult who suffers from an illogical fear which you would like to overcome, then it is possible to go ahead and do so without knowing what caused it in the first place. The Life Scripts contained in this chapter will give you the method; the time it takes will depend on the amount of time you are prepared to give to the process – but we are talking about weeks as opposed to years.

Without intending to make light of the very real distress caused by illogical fears, a phobia is one of the easiest things to overcome. And, what is more, you can overcome it completely and *forever*. (And it is untrue that, if the initial cause is not discovered, another fear will arise to take its place.)

There is no point in trying to use logic or common sense when dealing with your phobia. You may *know* that you are bigger than a spider, that it will not hurt you and that you have various methods of getting rid of it – but this knowledge does nothing to reduce the terror you feel when you encounter one. If logic was all it took, the problem would have been dealt with years ago.

The fear is rooted deep within your subconscious and, every time you experience it, the subconscious belief is reinforced. You cannot compel it to disappear; you have to work on it one stage at a time – and that is what this series of scripts is designed to do.

AGORAPHOBIA

This is a distressing condition which can ruin the life of the sufferer. If it is an extreme case, he may become a prisoner in his own home, unable to set foot outside without experiencing severe panic attacks. It can cause the agoraphobic to lose contact with friends and family; it can even destroy relationships as it is extremely difficult for the non-sufferer to understand the agonies experienced. However, with time and effort, agoraphobia can be completely overcome.

As you read the scripts below, you will see that the process is accomplished in relatively small stages. For them to be permanently effective, it is *essential* that you feel completely at ease with one before progressing to the next. So please don't feel tempted to proceed too rapidly as this may actually prevent a cure.

Do remember that each Life Script should be preceded

by the relaxation exercise already given to you. Also, you need to find a place to practise your technique where you feel completely safe – perhaps in your favourite chair, perhaps in bed.

Agoraphobia script – 1

I feel calm, relaxed and completely at ease. My body is free from tension and my breathing is regular. If I listen, I can hear the steady rhythm of my breathing. Whatever problems I may have in my daily life have been placed to one side to be considered later.

As I lie here, my eyes closed and my breathing slow and even, I imagine myself standing at my own front door. The door is still closed and I look at its shape and design. I see the handle, the hinges, the letter box – all those parts of the door with which I am familiar. I feel perfectly relaxed and comfortable.

I am aware that, in a moment, I am going to open my front door and look out into the garden. This thought does not trouble me at all because I feel so relaxed and because I know that what I am doing is only in my mind. I am in complete control.

Now I open the door and look out into the garden beyond. I am perfectly relaxed, my breathing is slow and even and I know that I do not have to step outside the door. I take in the details of the garden in front of the house – its shape and design and any plants there may be. I look at the path and the gate. I feel safe and secure because I am in control of my mind and I only see what I choose to see.

Still feeling quite relaxed and still breathing slowly and evenly, I remain standing inside my house but I look at what is beyond the front garden. I see the pavement and the road. I watch the people and the vehicles as they pass. I look up and see the sky, noting its colour and thinking of what this tells me about the weather.

Having surveyed the scene outside my front door, very slowly and in a controlled and deliberate way, I gently close the door. My whole being fills with joy as I realize that I have been able to look at the garden, the street and the sky without experiencing any negative feelings at all. I know that I can return to look at this scene again whenever I want and that I will always be able to do so with complete peace of mind.

This script should be used daily until the time comes when you feel comfortable about the idea of standing at your front door and looking out. This might take anything from a few days to two or three weeks – there is no 'right' or 'wrong' amount of time. When that time comes, practise your relaxation exercise and then go and open that door and look out into the garden (or whatever is there) beyond. You will experience no sense of panic – nor will you do so ever again. *BUT* please don't allow your sense of achievement to tempt you to do more than you have mentally rehearsed.

Suggested affirmations

- I can open my door and look out into my garden any time I want
- I am beginning to be in control of my life
- The world beyond my own four walls is a beautiful place.

Agaraphobia script – 2

I am relaxed and peaceful and eager to begin the next stage of my progress.

I visualize myself going to the front door and opening it as I have done so many times before –

both in my mind and in reality. I am confident that I shall experience only pleasure when I open the door; all fears previously attached to that action have now disappeared and will never return.

The door is open and I stand there for a few moments looking at the familiar scene. Now I decide how far I would like to go down the garden path. It might be just a few steps or it might be all the way to the gate. The choice is mine. I am in control of the situation and it causes me no anxiety because I know that I am doing all this in my imagination.

I take a single step outside the front door and pause, listening to the steady rhythm of my breathing, aware that I am calm and relaxed. Now, slowly and in a controlled fashion, I walk down the garden path – just to the point where I have decided to stop. I turn back to look at the house I have just left. I look towards the gate and the world beyond it. I feel a sense of joy because I know that soon that world will be mine.

When I have stood there for a few moments I turn and walk slowly and calmly back to the house again. I step inside, take one last look at the front garden and then gently close the door.

As with the previous script, practise this visualization until you are able to take those steps in reality.

Suggested affirmations

- I can leave the house and walk to my gate without any fear at all
- I am beginning to control my life more and more
- I am truly happy with my progress.

The third script helps you to progress even further. Provided you have worked slowly through the first two, you are extremely unlikely to suffer any sensation of panic when you venture further afield. However, because as much distress can be caused by the *fearful anticipation* of panic as by panic itself, this is a good stage at which to decide what you would do should that panic arise.

The majority of phobia sufferers dread two different aspects of a panic attack:

1. The sensation itself with its accompanying trembling, feeling of nausea, spinning head, etc.
2. The fact that they might look foolish in front of other people who will then go on to think less of them. Of course, in logical moments we all know that most people are so wrapped up in their own affairs that they probably won't notice a thing – certainly not that you are blushing, perspiring or showing some other symptom of anxiety. But the fears connected with a phobia are not logical and so the sufferer believes that his agony is visible to everyone.

Planning in advance just what you would do should you suffer an attack in public is often sufficient to ensure that such an attack never occurs – and that is what this next script is designed to help you achieve.

Agoraphobia script – 3

As I relax safely and comfortably, I think back over the success I have already had and the things I have done which I used not to be able to do. I have already proved to myself that, using the power of my own mind, I am able to be in control and to avoid any sensation of panic.

Although I know that this method of overcoming my anxiety works effectively, I have decided to plan how I will deal with the situation should an attack come upon me when I am in a public place or with other people.

I realize that, although I am always very conscious of my physical reactions to fear, other people are likely to be so concerned with what they are doing and thinking that they are unlikely to notice them. Statistics show that there are many, many phobia sufferers and yet I do not go around looking into the faces of strangers to see whether or not they are having an anxiety attack. Just like all those other people, I tend to be preoccupied with my own thoughts and actions.

(Knowing that I can now go to my front gate and beyond, I now imagine walking to the end of the road and entering the local shop to make a few purchases. As I visualize myself doing this, I am aware that I am totally relaxed and my breathing is slow and steady. I realize that this walk is only in my mind and that I am in complete control of the situation and so I feel not only calm and peaceful but also a sense of joy that I am able to do something which I used to feel was beyond me.

As I go into the shop, I see that there are several customers there already. In the past this would have made me panic but now, because I feel calm and at ease, I quietly wait my turn. Should I feel a sensation of anxiety rising within me, I shall simply stand still, pick up an item and look at it closely. To anyone else it will appear that I am studying it intently with a view to deciding whether or not to buy it. In reality, I shall hold the item while concentrating on regulating my breathing until it is once more slow and even.

Once I am calm again, I imagine myself making my purchases, paying for them, walking to the door of the shop and leaving. I make my way home again, feeling elated because I have progressed yet another step in ridding myself of the phobia for ever. I reach my own home, proud of my achievement.)

(Knowing that I can now go to my front gate and beyond, I imagine myself going for a walk to the local park – something I used to love but have not done for some time. Because this is taking place in my mind, I know that I am in complete control and can work at my own pace. I shall go as far into the park as I choose and I can retrace my steps whenever I want.

I visualize my walk in the park, noticing the flowers and the trees, full of joy because I am doing something I have wanted to do for so long. I see other people walking there and little children playing. Everything looks just as I remembered it – but so much better.

Should I reach a certain point and then begin to experience a sensation of anxiety, I shall simply stop and look around me as if taking in the sights, sounds and smells of the park. If there is a bench or chair nearby, I might sit on it. If there is a fence, I might lean against it. To anyone else my movements will look perfectly natural and it will only take a moment or two to regulate my breathing once more, after which I continue my walk.

I am in control of the situation so, once I feel I have walked for long enough, I turn around and start to make my way back home once more. I am so happy and so proud of myself for what I have achieved and I know that I can walk in the park any time I want and that my phobia is beginning to recede. And once it has gone, it will have vanished for ever.)

Suggested affirmations

- I am in control
- I know what I would do should I begin to feel anxious
- No one else will ever know if I feel uncomfortable
- I can overcome agoraphobia for ever.

Adapting the script above, you can learn to cope with any situation which normally causes you anxiety. Only you know which places cause you to feel agoraphobic, so naturally you will be able to personalize the script for your own benefit. In all the time I have worked as a hypnotherapist, I have never known this particular technique for dealing with agoraphobia to fail – provided of course the patient is willing to play his part and to practise frequently. Some people may take a little longer than others to overcome the phobia completely – but when you take into account the length of time they have usually been suffering, what difference does an extra week or two make?

CLAUSTROPHOBIA

Although a claustrophobia sufferer dreads different experiences to the agoraphobic, nonetheless the scripts used are similar in many respects.

Many situations may induce claustrophobic sensations but there are three which seem to be more common than any others. These are:

- fear of being in a lift
- fear of being in a large shop, particularly if nowhere near the door or window
- fear of being in someone else's house (or perhaps a restaurant, cinema, etc.).

For the purposes of the scripts which follow and the visualizations linked with them, I am assuming that in your home you have a cupboard under the stairs. I realize, of course, that this is not true of everyone but, once you have read and understood the scripts, you will see that you can adapt this to a shed, a garage – even a bathroom or toilet.

As with agoraphobia, it is essential when dealing with claustrophobia that you proceed slowly, making sure that you have successfully completed each part of the process before continuing to the next one. Please don't be tempted to hurry it as you will not succeed on a permanent basis and will only cause yourself to become disheartened. I cannot even tell you how long each stage should take as this varies from one individual to another and even from one step to another.

Claustrophobia script – 1

I have been relaxing for several moments and so my mind and my body are free from tension. My breathing is slow and regular and I feel quite calm and peaceful.

As I lie here, completely relaxed, I imagine myself going into the hall and walking to the door of the cupboard under the stairs. I look at the door, put my hand on the handle and pull the door open. I remain standing in the hall but bend forwards so that I can look inside the cupboard.

Because I know that I am doing this in my imagination only, my subconscious mind accepts that there is no reason for me to panic. I am in complete control of this visualization and can bring it to an end whenever I wish.

Having looked inside the cupboard and realized that this does not make me feel tense or anxious, I decide to take a step forward so that I am just inside it. If there is a light, I keep it on. If there is no light in the cupboard, I keep the light on in the hall. *I do not close the cupboard door* but leave it wide open so that I can see into the hall. I know that it will take just one large step for me to be outside the cupboard again. However, I feel so relaxed that I do not feel the need to take that step, even though I realize that I am in a confined space.

I spend a few moments concentrating on my steady breathing and then I reach out and pull the door a few inches towards me – stopping as soon as I feel that I want to. Once again I stop, feeling calm, relaxed and in control, aware of the regular rhythm of my breathing and the lack of tension in my body.

Now I close the door a few more inches, stopping at whatever point I wish. I am still relaxed and comfortable. If I feel that this visualization has gone far enough for today, I shall imagine pushing the door wide open again and stepping out into the hall before opening my eyes.

However, if I feel that I could close the door still further, I will continue to do so – a few inches at a time – until it is almost closed. At no time will I pull it so hard that the catch engages and it clicks closed; I will always know that all I have to do is give it one push and it will be wide open again.

The whole time I am aware that I feel calm and comfortable and completely without fear. I am in control of the situation.

When I have completed the visualization, I open my eyes, aware that I have done something in my imagination, the thought of which would in the past have caused me to experience discomfort. Yet on this occasion I realize that I experienced only peace and relaxation.

This script should be used regularly – at least once a day. On each occasion take the visualization as far as you wish. Sometimes you might not be able to imagine closing the door at all whereas at others you might feel that you could close it fully. After you have used it for some days – *and only when you feel ready* – you can try translating your visualization into reality. You should soon find that you are able to stand in that cupboard (or some equivalent place) without experiencing any panic at all.

Suggested affirmations

- I can stand in enclosed spaces
- There is always a way out.

For the purposes of the second script, I am going to use the example of being in a shop as this is something which affects so many people. Because escalators and staircases exist, it is possible to live without going in a lift but life is very difficult if you never go away from the door when you enter a shop. If your predominant fear involves some other situation which causes you to feel claustrophobic, you can substitute it for the one given. Or, having dealt with going into a shop or department store, you can use the same technique to deal with all other aspects of your claustrophobia.

Claustrophobia script – 2

I have already proved to myself that, by relaxing and imagining a certain situation, I can go on to succeed in being in that situation without feeling any anxiety. I am proud of myself for what I have achieved and I know that I am coming to the end of my time as a sufferer from claustrophobia. If I can stand in a cupboard with the door almost closed, I can certainly go into a brightly lit store.

So, aware once again that my mind and body are completely relaxed, I visualize myself entering a large shop. It has glass doors and large windows. I decide to wander through the shop to examine the goods but, because I am controlling this situation, I shall only ever go as far as I wish. At no time will I force myself to go beyond a point where I feel relaxed and comfortable.

I walk into the shop, stopping whenever I wish to look at the goods displayed there and to ensure that my breathing is slow and steady. Then I ask myself whether I wish to go further; if I feel that I do, I take a few more steps. If I do not wish to go further on this occasion, I look around and see how far I have come. I am really happy with the progress I have made.

I know that, because I am in control, I shall never feel anxiety or discomfort. To ensure that I remain in control, however, I decide what I would do should I begin to feel uncomfortable. I realize that all I need to do is turn around and retrace my steps until I reach the door once more so, should any anxious feelings manifest themselves, I would stand still until my breathing became regular and even and then slowly and steadily walk towards the door of the shop.

I am relaxed, happy and proud of myself.

Use this script until you are quite at ease with the idea of walking into a shop and then put it into practice. To begin with, do it on an occasion when you do not really need to buy anything specific so that you can concentrate on the feeling of satisfaction as you go deeper and deeper into the shop's interior.

Suggested affirmations

- I can enter any shop I wish
- My claustrophobia no longer exists
- I am free.

FEAR OF SPIDERS

There are about 130 listed phobias and obviously it is not possible to give a script for each one. But the technique is similar in each case and you will easily adapt the scripts which follow to deal with your own particular fears. I have selected fear of spiders (arachnophobia) because it is one experienced by so many people.

When you have a dread of any creature – for example, spider, bird, mouse or snake – remember that the aim is not to make you suddenly love it; indeed, you may never like it or want to touch it. What we are trying to do is help you rid yourself of the (often illogical) extreme panic the very sight of one causes in you.

You know that a spider cannot hurt you. You are so much bigger than it is that you could walk away, flick it with a newspaper – or even dispose of it in a far less pleasant way. You know that it will not bite or sting you (we are not talking here about scorpions and similar creatures where a healthy caution is advisable but about the common house or garden spider). Have you ever stopped to wonder what it is that you find so frightening?

Quite often – especially in women – this fear stems from early childhood. At one time little girls would scream and shudder at the sight of any creature which wriggled or was considered unpleasant to look at. And, of course, the more they encouraged each other in this screaming and shuddering, the more the idea became fixed in their subconscious minds that these really were frightening monsters to be avoided at all costs.

But, whatever the initial cause of the phobia, it is quite a simple one to dispel. At no time is aversion therapy the answer. There is nothing to be gained by compelling yourself (without any preparatory mental rehearsal) to pick up the offending creature. In fact, if you were to do this you would probably increase the phobia considerably.

The first stage is to be able to think about the dreaded spider without feelings of revulsion and this is what is covered in the first script. If, in preparation, you could obtain a book which contains several pictures of common spiders, so much the better. You don't have to open the book before practising the first script.

Fear of spiders script – 1

My mind and body are completely relaxed, my breathing is slow and regular and a feeling of peace pervades my being. I know that I am choosing to take control of an area of my life where previously I have been out of control. At all stages I shall work only at a pace with which I feel comfortable and relaxed.

I have in my possession a book which I know contains pictures of common spiders, although I have not yet opened the book to look at those pictures. I imagine picking up that book and holding it, still closed, in my hand. I feel its texture, see the colour of the cover and read the title. And all the time I feel perfectly calm because what I am doing is only in my imagination and I can stop whenever I wish.

I visualize flicking quickly through the pages, not stopping to look at any one in detail. Even though I may not see any picture clearly, they are registering on my subconscious – and yet I still feel calm, relaxed and peaceful. Now I study the index of the book to discover on which page there is a picture of a common spider. I turn to this page and look at the picture. At no time do I feel any fear or revulsion – although I know that, if I did, all I have to do is close the book again.

I continue to look at the picture of the spider and imagine myself running my fingers over the page. If there is any printed information about the spider, I find my eyes drawn to it and I begin to read. Some of the facts are fascinating and were quite unknown to me.

Now, having studied the picture for some time, I close the book and put it down before concentrating once again on the feeling of deep relaxation and opening my eyes.

When you have practised using this script for some time, pick up the book, find an appropriate page and look at the picture of the common spider. You will feel no aversion, no fear. (You may decide you think it is ugly – but that is quite another matter.)

Suggested affirmations

- I can look at pictures of common spiders whenever I want
- A spider is more frightened of me than I am of it
- Spiders are God's creatures too.

Fear of spiders script – 2

I have looked at pictures of spiders in a book and I have learned about their lives and habitat. I can do that any time I wish without experiencing any anxiety at all.

Now, feeling relaxed and comfortable, I imagine myself strolling in my garden (in the park) (down the street). I look at the hedges or by wooden buildings to see if I can see a spider's web. When I discover a web, I am intrigued by the intricacy and regularity of its design and by the fact that all webs are constructed in precisely the same way.

Still aware that I am relaxed and that my breathing is steady and even, I look around to see whether I can see the spider itself. I observe it sitting quietly on the outer ring of the web; it does not move. I look at it for a few moments before going on my way.

I am happy that there was no anxiety aroused by seeing that spider and know that I am now in control of that situation. I can be equally in control should a spider come into the house. I will always have a choice as to what I do about it. I can simply turn and walk out of the room. I can roll up a newspaper and flick the spider away. I can cover it with an upturned glass and leave it for someone else to deal with. The decision will always be mine and, therefore, I will always be the one in control. Knowing this, I have no need to feel panic at the sight of a spider ever again.

You may not be able to arrange for a spider to pay you a visit but, having worked with this script, you can certainly go out and look for one. Remember, no one is asking you to love it or even to touch it if you prefer not to. All you want is to be able to face one without experiencing any anxiety or panic and this you will be able to do.

Suggested affirmations

- I can look at a spider whenever I want
- I will always be in control of the situation
- Spiders create webs which are things of beauty.

By the way, did you know that spiders are far more civilized than many human beings? If two spiders each decide that they would like to take possession of a particular web, they do not fight. Each one stands on an outside arm of the web and each plucks the thread itself. From this they are able to tell which of them is the stronger – and the weaker one simply goes away. Spiders don't have wars!

4

Dealing with Emotions

Our emotions need careful handling. If we were all capable of being calm and logical on demand, we would have far fewer problems. We would be able to 'be sensible', 'snap out of it', 'look on the bright side' – and all those other positive things we may be told to do by people who are not feeling what we are feeling.

No one ever altered their emotional state by being told – or even telling themselves – to do so. And, painful though those emotions may sometimes be, they are what makes us the complex, caring creatures we are.

There are, however, people who find themselves trapped in an emotional morass from which there seems to be no escape and which effectively prevents them getting on with the rest of their lives. In such cases help – and it can be self-help – is needed to free them and allow them to progress in a positive way.

I have selected three main headings for the Life Scripts in the first part of this chapter. These are the ones we all experience at some time in our lives:

- Coping with bereavement
- The break-up of a relationship
- Feeling guilty.

BEREAVEMENT

Isn't it strange that, when young, we are taught how to do all sorts of things which we may or may not have to put into practice at a later date yet no one ever tells us how to deal with the one thing we are undoubtedly going to have to face at some time – the death of someone we care for.

Whether that death is expected or whether it comes as a complete surprise, there is a range of emotions to be experienced – and it is truly important that you allow yourself to experience each of them without trying to resist them or hide them from yourself or other people.

Naturally you will feel sorrow if the person who has died is someone you cared for deeply. This is true even when the death is a happy release for someone who has been suffering the pain and distress of a progressive disease. It has been said that we cry for ourselves and not for the person who has gone and this is probably true – but there is nothing wrong in doing so. If you are sad, if you regret what has gone or what can now never be, if you feel suddenly alone – then go ahead and cry. It is a natural and necessary release and to try to stifle the tears would only cause problems at a later date.

Another of the natural emotions experienced after a loss is that of anger. That anger may take many forms – you may feel angry with the person who has died because they have gone away and left you behind. It does not matter that they didn't choose to do so or that you might feel you are being selfish – you have a right to experience that anger. It may manifest itself as an anger towards other people – people who have not died or who still have *all* their loved ones around them. Or you might feel rage at the sun for shining or the flowers for blooming when all the world ought to be feeling as unhappy as you do right now. These feelings too are part of the bereavement process and you should allow yourself to experience and acknowledge them. They will pass in time.

Perhaps the hardest emotion to come to terms with is that of guilt. Sorrow and anger dissipate – or at least grow mellow with the passing of time – but the effects of guilt can linger for years unless you face up to it and do something to alleviate it.

There may be many reasons for these feelings of guilt; perhaps you were not there when the end came and you feel you should have been; perhaps you regret words spoken or unspoken and deeds done or not done. It is usually the smallest things which cause these feelings. A woman who came to see me for bereavement counselling had nursed her husband through a terminal illness with love, patience and tenderness. The night before he died he had called out for a drink of water and she had gone to fetch one but had done so with bad grace, muttering to herself bad-temperedly as her feet met the cold kitchen floor. When morning came and the man died, his wife did not remember the months of loving care; all she could think of was the fact that she had felt resentful when giving him what turned out to be his last drink of water.

Sometimes, of course, the guilt has a far more deep-rooted cause. Perhaps there has been bad feeling in the relationship. Possibly angry words have been spoken or a bitter silence has existed. There may be guilty feelings because love was not present between the parties and, once one of them has died, the other has to continue living with that knowledge.

Marie's father had been strict and authoritarian with no visible signs of tenderness. His temper had been violent and his punishment of his daughter often physical. As soon as she was old enough, Marie had left home never to return. Although she kept in touch with her mother, the only feelings she harboured for her father were bitter resentment and she refused to have any contact with him. Just before the old man died, her mother had written to her and asked her to come to the hospital. Marie was shocked to find that the person she remembered as rigid and frightening had become frail and elderly with rheumy eyes and shaking hands. After he died, Marie was unable to get this picture out of her mind and she began to doubt her own memories of her unhappy childhood. This in turn caused her to feel guilty for failing to have contact with her father – or indeed to love him.

Of course a person does not become sweet and lovable

just by growing old or ill. And there is no law which states that we have a duty to love those who were harsh or cruel to us simply because they are our parents. Yet inside most of us is the subconscious belief that we *must* love our mother and father, whether they were cruel or kind. When life or circumstances do not permit us to experience this love, the inner self takes the blame and causes us to feel guilty.

The two scripts which follow are designed with different purposes in mind. The first is to help you overcome the initial grief and come to terms with the fact that the person has died. The second script should be used only in those circumstances where there has been bad feeling or misunderstanding between you and the person who has died. As always, each script should be preceded by the relaxation exercise given earlier.

Bereavement script – 1

As I relax and allow a sensation of peace and comfort to flow over me, I realize that it is quite all right for me to experience the range of emotions I have felt since your passing. I know that, when I cry, I cry mostly for myself and my loss. Whatever comes after this life, you can no longer experience any pain – mental or physical. And so, although I am unhappy at this moment, I realize that the sorrow will recede with the passing of time. I know that you would not wish me to continue grieving for ever and that the greatest compliment I can pay to your memory is to remember your life with joy and love.

As I relax here and think about you, I choose to picture you in happy times. I remember an occasion when it was a pleasure simply to be with you. I allow one memory to follow another in my mind, recalling the smiles, the laughter, the joy. If these memories cause tears to flow, I allow them to do so, knowing that they are nature's way of helping to heal the wound. But, even amid my tears, I find myself able to smile at what was amusing and to take pleasure in the fact that I knew you and we were part of each other's lives.

I loved you in your lifetime and I continue to love you now. I realize that you loved me too, whatever my faults and failings. We do not love someone only when they are perfect. I have not stopped loving you just because you have died – and I know that you have not stopped loving me.

I shall sit here for as long as I wish, allowing the images to come into my mind, one after another, and then, when I feel ready, I shall quietly open my eyes and feel the sensation of peace.

Suggested affirmations

- I am allowed to grieve
- I can think of happy times
- Thank you for letting me be part of your life and for being part of mine.

The purpose of the next Life Script is to allow you to complete any 'unfinished business' with the person who has died. You are going to have the opportunity to go through a role-play experience in your imagination. This will help you relegate to the past any residual guilt or anger. You will be able to say all those things which were never said, secure in the knowledge that you cannot hurt the feelings of the person to whom you are speaking because, if they have entered the spiritual life, they will understand. Just as an adult can understand what a small child says in a fit of rage, without taking offence from it, so too will the person you are going to speak to.

Perhaps you feel that you were the wronged one, that someone who should have loved you, cared for you and been good to you, failed to do so. If that is the case you will be able to ask them why they acted (or failed to act) as they did and your subconscious mind will supply you with the answer. You see, even if there was hurt and misunderstanding, somewhere deep within you is a realization of *why* they behaved in such a way. This does not necessarily excuse their actions but it does allow you to forgive and then – even more important – to free yourself from the pain of the past.

Bereavement script – 2

I am in a peaceful, tranquil state, ready to complete any unfinished business left over from the past so that I can be free of feelings of guilt, distress or anger.

I see you in my mind, not as you were when you died, but as I remember you at a time when your words, actions or attitude had the greatest effect upon me. And I am going to use this time to talk honestly to you – to tell you of my feelings and emotions towards you. I know that from your current position of increased knowledge and awareness, you will not be hurt by anything I say but will understand, possibly for the first time, the emotions I feel and the reasons behind them.

I can choose whether to speak the words aloud or to imagine speaking them; whichever I do, you will understand them perfectly. If I feel the need to criticize you or to ask your forgiveness, you will understand. If I ask you *why* you treated me as you did, you will understand that too – and if I listen to my deep subconscious your answers will come to me. (*At this point, continue with the inner conversation, using your own words and experiencing the response. Take as long as you wish before continuing.*)

The fact that we may have begun to understand each other a little more brings a sense of peace to my mind. I know that it may be necessary to repeat this process in order to deal with all the emotions which existed between us. I also know that, one day, it will be possible to let you go and to say goodbye to each other in a state of true understanding.

Whether you need to use the second script more than once will depend on the depth of your feelings (good or bad) for the person who has died. But each time you use it you will feel a little better about the past and freer to head towards the future.

Suggested affirmations

- Now I can be totally honest with you
- We are beginning to understand each other
- I can let the past go.

THE BREAK-UP OF A RELATIONSHIP

We all experience many different sorts of relationships, so the scripts in this section do not simply apply to husbands/wives, boy and girlfriends or lovers. A rift can occur in the relationship between parent and child, brother and sister or good friends. The emotions felt are dramatic in each case – whether or not you were the instigator of the parting.

If the other person was the one to cause the rift, you will probably feel rejected. This in turn can lead to low self-esteem – 'he (or she) left me because I am not lovable; that must be right, so I will never find anyone else to love me.' Or you may feel anger – how *dare* anyone treat you like this! In either case, you are likely to experience (in various proportions) regret, loneliness, fear, bitterness and self-doubt.

There are two scripts in this section. The first is to be used when there has been a break-up between loving partners, whether married, living together or on the threshold of a commitment – and when the split is irrevocable. The second script is designed to help you deal with a damaged relationship within the family unit – to repair it if that is what you wish or, if that is not possible, to come to terms with the ending of it. Your parent or your child cannot cease to be so and, in many cases, provided there is the genuine desire on both sides, the relationship can be repaired. However, there may be instances where the pain inflicted is so great that it is better for the relationship to come to an end. In this case, help is still needed to come to terms with the decision made.

Just as in the case of a bereavement, if you have been abandoned by someone whose love you had come to depend on, it is necessary to acknowledge your feelings before you can let them go. Of course you will feel hurt; of course you will feel unhappy; of course you will sometimes feel lonely – all that is quite natural. What you must not do is permit those feelings to become so ingrained that they cause you to have a lowered opinion of yourself or to feel fearful about the future. The script which follows (and which should be used after practising the relaxation technique) is designed to help you.

Relationship break-up script – 1

I am coming to terms with being without someone about whom I have cared deeply. This causes many deep emotions but I realize that it is normal to experience them and, indeed, if I did not feel them it would mean that the relationship between us was never a strong one.

It is quite all right to feel sad, to feel a sense of loss, to feel loneliness. Even though I may be experiencing pain at the moment, I know that it will pass and that I will find life to be good again. I will allow myself the temporary indulgence of wallowing in my feelings if I feel the need to do so. But I know that it must only be temporary and that soon I must begin to live my life to the full again.

There is no stigma attached to being alone; it would be far worse to spend my time and waste my love on someone with whom I did not feel right, whether because I could not truly love them or because they could not love me in return.

Whether I was the instigator of the break-up of the relationship or whether it was forced upon me, I will not allow it to affect my self-image. I am a warm and loving person and I deserve a warm and loving relationship. Anything less would be a betrayal of my own self and would eventually damage my self-esteem.

I accept that what has gone has vanished for ever and I shall not waste my time trying to rekindle a flame which has been extinguished, whether or not it was of my choosing. I am grateful to the relationship for the good times we experienced and those are what I choose to remember. If I allow myself to return again and again to the painful moments, I shall only harm my own future.

When the immediate pain is over, I shall ask myself what I have learned from this relationship. If I caused it to come to an end because of some mistake on my part, I shall know what to avoid in future. If the other person was never going to be the right one for me, I shall ask myself what led me to choose them in the first place and what I can do to ensure that I do not become involved with someone similar in future. If I believed that all was going well and the split was thrust upon me, I shall wonder why I did not realize that the other person was unhappy and falling out of love. Any or all of these thoughts will lead to an improvement in my self-knowledge and, for that reason alone, the relationship will have served a purpose.

I look forward to the day when I can love again and be loved in the way I would choose. But, until that day comes, I shall appreciate the sense of freedom which now surrounds me. I have the freedom to do what I wish and to live life as fully as I choose. There is a whole world to be experienced – even if I never go more than a few miles from my own home. That world is full of places to see and things to do. There are new people to meet, some of whom may become my friends. I have people around me who care about me and I shall take the time to cherish those people and spend time with them.

I am going to begin now, as soon as I have finished this exercise, by writing down three things I would really like to do during the coming days. And I am going to make sure that I do them.

Suggested affirmations

- I have learned something from the relationship which has ended
- I am a worthwhile person who deserves to be loved
- Life is to be lived – starting now!

Relationship break-up script – 2

As I contemplate the rift which has arisen between me and someone to whom I would expect to feel close, I know that I must experience and acknowledge the emotions I feel.

These emotions are likely to be mixed. At times I will feel sadness, at times I may be angry. Perhaps the rift has come as a shock or perhaps it is something which was the inevitable result of long-term bad feeling. Whatever the cause, it is always sad when two people whom the world would expect to get on well are unable to do so.

I have to ask myself some questions so that I can

know which way to proceed from here. Do I want to repair the damage and mend the relationship? Do I feel that the gulf is so wide and the hurt so great that I would not want to repair it under any circumstances? Only I can decide and I must be completely honest with myself and not be influenced by what others think I should do.

In my imagination, I picture myself as I shall be in five years time if the relationship has been rekindled. Am I happy? Is it what I want? Now I picture myself as I shall be in five years time if nothing is done to heal the rift. Is this better? Am I more or less happy? As I relax and allow my subconscious to create the images, I will know instinctively (as opposed to logically) whether I want to repair the damaged relationship.

(I have decided that I wish to heal the rift and become close again to (*insert name*). Having made that decision, I am not going to wait to see whether they are going to make the first move. I realize that the relationship is a worthwhile one and I do not intend to let my pride stand in the way of repairing it. I shall spend some time relaxing and allowing myself to consider the various ways I could go about repairing the damage. Only after doing this shall I select what I consider to be the best way. Then I shall waste no time in setting it in motion.

I realize that the relationship will be on a different footing. The rift which has occurred between us, however temporary it may be, means that we have both changed a little and so will begin as slightly different people. If we are both wiser and more understanding, the relationship will be even better and more worthwhile than before and more rewarding for each of us.

I am looking forward to the future and to the warmth of feeling between us.)

(I have decided that the rift between us is too great ever to be healed; indeed I do not wish it to be healed and I prefer to have no more contact with (*insert name*) than is essential. I can only come to this conclusion in a calm and relaxed state; if it arose as the result of a fit of temper, I could not trust my decision.

It does not matter why I have come to this conclusion – only that I have reached it. Having done so, I shall not allow myself to be influenced by other people. Only I can know what is right for me to do.

Deciding not to have anything more to do with someone does not mean that I have to feel hatred, dislike or anger towards them. That would achieve nothing and would only be harmful to me. If I let the person go, I choose to let the feelings go too.

Nothing need be forever and no door needs to be permanently closed and barred. If I should ever, for whatever reason, change my mind, I could always try to take steps to heal the rift some time in the future.)

Having made my decision, I feel so much lighter and freer from tension. I am able to let go all the negative emotion which was involved and go forwards positively towards the future.

Suggested affirmations

- I have made my own decision about the future of the relationship
- It is up to me to make the first move
- I am free of negative emotion.

If you have come to the second conclusion, that is, that you no longer wish to have contact with the person in question, that should mean that they no longer have the power to hurt you. You cannot always ensure that you never actually see them again, particularly if they are related to you or live in the same town. However, if they no longer have power over you, it should not be difficult to be civil should the occasion arise. If you find this impossible, then you have not freed yourself from their influence and need to do more work, using the script and the affirmations.

FEELINGS OF GUILT

There are so many reasons why we might feel guilty – although guilt is one of the most destructive of emotions because it leaves the sufferer feeling insecure and unworthy.

It could be, of course, that someone has done something in the past about which he has reason to feel guilty. This could be anything from hurting another person's feelings to committing a crime. Once the deed has been done, feeling guilty is a pointless and ineffectual emotion. It is far more positive to do any or all of the following:

- acknowledge your mistake
- experience regret
- make amends if this is possible
- determine to learn from your past failure
- resolve not to do it again.

And that is all you can do. No purpose is served by spending the rest of your life wallowing in guilt – nothing is achieved, no lessons are learned and no reparation is made.

Everyone has done things they regret at some time so you are not alone in having made a mistake. Use the script which follows to help you to come to terms with your own error – whatever it may be – and to learn from it.

Guilt script – 1

I am enjoying the peaceful sensation of true relaxation and I would like to be able to experience that peace in my everyday life without the feelings of guilt which have been pursuing me.

Whatever my mistake in the past – however great it may have been – I can do nothing to delete it. But no good can be served by my continued self-inflicted torment; it does not undo anything which has been said or done.

I acknowledge to myself that I was wrong and that I regret what I did, particularly if it caused harm or distress, directly or indirectly, to any other person. If there is any way in which I can make amends for what I have done, I will have the courage to do so. But there is no point in talking about what I have done if there is no specific advantage other than relieving my own feelings. If I think it will help me to understand how I feel, then when I have finished working with this Life Script, I shall write a letter to the person or people I have wronged – a letter which will never be sent but which I can destroy whenever I wish.

I realize that all failure is an opportunity to learn and develop. From now on, I intend to look upon my past error as part of the learning process of my life. It has taught me that, when I feel I have done something wrong, it makes my life miserable. This indicates that I am not the wicked person I may have been considering myself but just an ordinary human being who made a mistake. I can prove this to myself by resolving never to find myself in the same position again and, if I cannot make actual reparation for what I did in the past, to do so by behaving differently in the future.

Understanding myself in this way and making this resolution allows the weight of guilt to be lifted from me. I no longer have need of its negativity and can go forward to live life in a positive way.

Suggested affirmations

- I am sorry for what I did
- Mistakes are part of the learning process

- I shall not make the same mistake again – so I have no need to continue feeling guilty.

There are some people, of course, who feel guilty when there is no real cause. If this applies to you, you need to ask yourself why you feel this way. Were you always brought up to think that you were not good enough? Did someone always lay the blame for everything on you? Is there somebody who is so insecure that they need to criticize you constantly – and have you been so worn down by this criticism that you have come to accept it as truth?

You were not born with a tendency to feel guilty. It was inflicted on you somewhere along the way. And – what is even more important – you *allowed* it to happen. This is quite understandable as it probably began when you were very young. But *you do not have to allow it to go on any longer*. You have it in your power to put a stop to the situation and the script which follows will help you.

It could be that there is someone around who actively works at making you feel guilty. The type of person who says things like, 'If you really loved me you would . . .' or 'You go and enjoy yourself; don't worry about me.' This person is to be pitied; their own lack of inner confidence compels them to try to exert their power over you in this way. *But you do not have to let them succeed.* It will not help the development of their self-esteem – and it certainly won't do yours any good either.

There are two very effective ways of dealing with someone who sets out to make you feel guilty. If you can learn to see them as a pathetic figure, they will lose their power over you. Or you can learn to find them amusing by playing mental games when in their company – 'I wonder how long it will be before he tries to make me feel guilty' or 'Let's see how many different ways she can do it in ten minutes.' Even if you don't say a word, either of these methods puts you in control of the situation – and once you are in control, their ability to make you feel guilty has gone.

Guilt script – 2

Because I am relaxed with my mind and my body free from tension, I am able to see things more clearly. I realize that I accept feelings of guilt when there is no real reason for me to do so. I know that I am not a bad person – so why am I so ready to believe that I am always the one in the wrong?

(Perhaps I need to think about my past and to consider whether there was someone who, when I was very young, consistently told me that I was inferior in some way or that I was lacking in ability. If I can recall such a person I can see that it was their own sense of inferiority which caused them to behave in such a way. No one who has a reasonable sense of their own identity and worth has the need to hurt or belittle other people. Those words which caused me pain in the past have no power over me now that I can see the pathetic situation which caused them to be spoken. I may choose to feel pity or contempt for the speaker but, in either case, they have lost their ability to make me feel negative in either my present or my future life.)

(I realize that much of my present guilt is being deliberately caused by (*insert name*). For some reason (s)he has the need to cause me distress by making me feel guilty. I appreciate that no one would do such a thing unless they had a desperate need to feel powerful and in control – and that such a desperate need would not exist if they did not really feel unloved and inferior. The realization that this is how they truly feel destroys their ability to exert power over me.

I can choose how I react to such manipulation. I might simply decide to ignore it, remaining calm and polite and not allowing the words to inflict harm. Indeed, (*insert name*) is to be pitied – and no one I find pathetic can cause me to feel guilty. I might choose to find the situation amusing. Even if I say nothing to them, I can play games in my mind by keeping score of the number of guilt-inducing comments they make or the time it takes for them to make the first one. No one I find amusing has the power to make me feel guilty.)

From this moment onwards I am in control of the situation. I realize that I will only experience needless guilt if I allow myself to do so – and I choose not to allow it.

Use this script regularly until the negative feelings have left you. It is possible that they will return from time to time, especially in the early days and particularly if triggered by some specific incident. You can immediately counteract any sense of guilt by returning to the script and repeating it as often as needed.

Suggested affirmations

- I refuse to allow myself to be manipulated
- No one can make me feel guilty unless I give them permission to do so.
- Freedom from guilt is freedom to live my own life.

Until this point, this chapter has dealt with negative emotions and how to overcome them. But of course we experience positive emotions too – although we tend to pay these less attention. But positive feelings, such as joy or love, are so precious that we should do all we can to hold on to them and to store them carefully in our memories so that we can return to them, re-experiencing the sensation, whenever we wish.

JOY

It is very rare for someone never to have experienced joy. Even among those of my patients who come from tragic or miserable backgrounds, there have been moments of gladness – frequently brought about by quite trivial things. One woman, whose life has been difficult from the very beginning, remembered the sensation of stroking a horse in a nearby field on her way to school each morning. A man who had been raised in conditions of extreme poverty recalled the intense pleasure of placing his cold feet on a warm hot water bottle in his childhood bed.

Most of us are fortunate enough to have even more joyful sensations to recall – but how seldom we do so. The script which follows is designed to help you recall such moments and to recreate the accompanying emotion whenever you wish. Naturally this can be helpful when you encounter a difficult period in your life – but don't just save it for such occasions. Why not get into the habit of feeling joyful just for the wonderful lift it can give to your life at any time?

Joy script

I have made a conscious decision to put more joy into my life. There will be times when this will be easy because the existing situation will be one which induces joy. But, even at times when all around me seems negative, I can recreate the emotion of joy and this will help me to remember that, once the difficult time is over, I can be joyful again.

When I was young, simple things could make me joyful. As I relax now, I allow my mind to go back to my childhood. However good or bad it may have been in general terms, I know that, as a child, there were times when I experienced great pleasure. I am going to allow my subconscious to bring back one or more of those memories.

I am going to spend the next few moments looking at that memory in my mind in as much detail as possible. What could I see, hear, feel, smell or taste which brought me so much pleasure? Once

I have thought about it, I am going to allow my subconscious to feel that pleasure again. Whenever I have the desire to experience the sense of joy in the future, all I will have to do is remember that childhood image and I shall immediately begin to feel happy, optimistic and positive.

I realize that, at any stage in life, I am likely to have problems or difficult situations to deal with – but this does not mean that I should not be able to feel positive or find things to be joyful about, even at such times.

It is important to live for the present moment. I can do nothing to alter the past and, although I can make plans and decisions, I cannot entirely control the future. But I am responsible for my feelings at this instant. And joyousness is contagious; the more I can pass on to others, the more I will help them to feel positive about their own lives.

As I relax, the remembered image is growing clearer and the pleasurable emotions connected with it are becoming stronger. This is something I can do to improve the way I feel about my life at any time I wish.

That script is not designed to make you less aware of your problems or less capable of doing anything about them. But, even at times of difficulty, a remembered sensation of joy will help you to be more positive about what is going on around you. And, of course, you do not have to stick only to one past image; there is nothing to stop you building up a complete 'mental photograph album' so that you can turn to which page pleases you most.

Suggested affirmations

- I have some good memories which I can call to mind whenever I wish
- I deserve to experience joy

- The more positive I feel, the more I will be able to help others feel positive too.

LOVE

Perhaps the most positive emotion of all, love can make us feel better both physically and emotionally. There are many different kinds of love; there is the love we feel for our children, our friends, our lovers. There is the love we feel for mankind, for animals, for the world. There is the love we feel for God (or Spirit or whatever other name you care to use). Each kind of love is important and, although we may not be fortunate enough to experience all of them at the same time, there is an unbounded supply around us and the more we give, the more we are likely to receive in return. And, whatever life may be throwing at you, it is so much easier to cope with if you feel that you are loved.

Even when we know that the people around us love us, if that emotion is not expressed, it is easy to doubt it at times when we are feeling negative. Bearing that in mind, surely it must be important for us to remind others of our love for them – by words, by touch, by giving them our time.

This script will help you to become aware of all the love around you – the love you have to give and the love you can receive. As always, it should follow on from the relaxation technique.

Love script

As I relax, I let my mind wander back to my child-hood and I think about the love I felt then. Perhaps the love I felt for others of my family, perhaps for a pet or even a favourite doll or teddy bear. As a child I did not worry about whether or not that love was returned; I gave it unconditionally. Now I allow that sensation of love to fill my whole being, warming and tender. I am still that person; I still have a great deal of love to give.

I have also received love in my life – the love of family, of friends, of an animal. Whether or not those people are near me today, that love does not change – it still surrounds me. Even if one or more of them has died, I have the memory of their love to keep me warm and cherished and, just as I can continue to love someone who is no longer alive, there is no reason why they should stop loving me just because we cannot see each other.

Because I understand the importance of knowing you are loved, I shall make sure that I always let those I love realize how I feel. I will tell them and I will show them by giving them my time and my attention. I realize that the more love I am able to give, the more I am likely to receive.

I shall not forget to love myself – a very important form of love and yet one which is so often ignored. I know that, like every other human being, I have faults, but we do not love only perfection. Real love is given unconditionally, no matter what the faults in the recipient. So I can love myself, with all my imperfections. And the more I experience this love, the more I shall be able to work to change any aspect with which I am not happy.

No matter what happens to me during my life, I shall always have this reserve of remembered love, self-love and freely given love to draw upon. This will help me to cope with negative times and enhance positive ones.

Suggested affirmations

- I know what it is like to be loved
- I love myself
- I will give love wherever I can – and I will be sure to tell and show others that I love them.

5

Helping Recovery

There are many ways in which you can use Life Scripts to speed your own recovery from various conditions. You can help to reduce pre-menstrual tension, disperse attacks of asthma, migraine or anxiety and recover quickly from illness or surgery.

PAIN

It is possible to use scripts to overcome pain – but you must be extremely careful how and when you do so. Pain is often there for a reason; it serves as a warning that all is not as it should be. If you simply take it away without finding out what the underlying cause is, you could be allowing a condition to deteriorate.

For example, a pain in your head could be nothing more nor less than a simple headache, resulting perhaps from stress, overwork or loud noise. But it could also be a sign that your eyesight needs to be tested or even, in extreme cases, that you have a brain tumour. You can see, therefore, how dangerous it would be merely to remove that pain without first investigating it.

Pain also reminds us not to overdo things. If you are recovering from a broken arm, the pain you feel will prevent you from trying to lift heavy weights or use the arm more than is suitable at whatever stage of recovery you have reached. It is for this reason that many doctors will not prescribe painkillers at this point – the pain is necessary to prevent you doing anything foolish or using the limb too much too soon.

So, please bear those thoughts in mind before working with one of the scripts which follow and which are designed to remove pain. Let me give you a few examples of people I have known who have used pain dispersal scripts both effectively and appropriately:

- Pauline became so anxious about her forthcoming driving test that she developed headaches as a result of the tension. She consulted her doctor and optician, both of whom gave her a clean bill of health, although the doctor did comment that she seemed to be under a great deal of stress in general and this was being exacerbated by her apprehension about the driving test. As the date of the test drew nearer, Pauline's headaches increased in frequency and intensity. Had they continued, she felt that she would not even have been fit enough to take the test. She successfully used an appropriate Life Script to eliminate the headaches altogether.

- James was a successful businessman who, some years earlier, had suffered an injury to his back which resulted in the fusion of several of the lower vertebrae. Since that time he had been in constant pain, although still relatively mobile. He found that he could cope with this during the day when he had so many things to think about, but could not get to sleep at night when there was nothing to distract his mind from the pain he was experiencing. And this lack of sleep was causing him to become tired, irritable and unable to think clearly during the day. With his doctor's approval, James worked with one of the following scripts which, although it did not remove the pain entirely, converted it into a dull ache which was not sufficient to prevent him sleeping.

- Anthony was a young man of thirty who sadly suffered from cancer. It had spread so rapidly through his body that he knew nothing could be done and he only had months to live. He had come to terms with the situation and was determined to enjoy those last months but he found that the painkillers administered were so strong that he was unable to speak or think clearly – and in fact slept most of the time. Before I ever met him, he had therefore chosen not to take them any more. Like James, he was able to cope relatively well during the day but told me that he was unable to sleep at night unless he drank about half a bottle of vodka. He did not want his last few months to be like this and so he learned to use a script to reduce the pain to a bearable level.

There are two suggested scripts for reducing pain and it is quite possible that one will suit you better than the other. So try them both and then use the one you prefer. But do give each a fair chance; try it for at least a week before rejecting it and going on to the other one. Of course, you may be quite happy to use a combination of the two – or even, once you have mastered the technique, to create another of your own. As always, the scripts should follow on from your usual relaxation exercise.

Pain reduction script – 1

I am aware that I am very relaxed and that my breathing is slow and regular. Just for a moment I am going to listen to the rhythm of my breathing, allowing it to fill my whole being.

I know that I have a pain in my body and I know that either no cause can be found other than stress or that the cause is known and I can do myself no harm by dispersing the pain.

As I breathe evenly, I am going to concentrate as hard as I can upon the area of pain. As I do so, I am going to visualize that pain as a hard, red ball within me. If I find it difficult to keep my concentration focussed upon that one spot, I can just place my hand gently over the area and allow the warmth from my hand to remind me of its location.

Now, working very slowly – an inch or two at a time – I visualize that hard, red ball of pain moving away from its original area. Gradually it moves itself inside my body until it comes to the nearest limb, be that arm or leg. Slowly, very slowly, I imagine it moving down that (arm) (leg) until it reaches my (fingers) (toes).

At this point I visualize the hard, red ball disintegrating into millions of tiny pieces, each one like a fine particle of dust. In my imagination I see that dust passing slowly along my (fingers) (toes) until it is able to flow out of the tips of them.

Now that the hard, red ball of pain has been completely eliminated from my body, I think back to that area where it began and realize that I am now free from pain in that part of my body. I relax again, breathing slowly and regularly, confident in the knowledge that I can use this script to reduce or eliminate pain whenever I wish.

Suggested affirmations

- I can control and eliminate pain
- Pain is a hard, red ball which can be completely destroyed.

When using this script, or the one which follows, it is very important to relax as thoroughly as possible first. Not only does this make the visualization both easier and more effective, but a tensed muscle will always experience more pain than a relaxed one. Think of injections. Although no one really likes having them, if you can relax as the needle is inserted you feel far less discomfort than if your muscles are tense.

Pain reduction script – 2

As I relax, breathing slowly and evenly, I imagine that I am walking through a pleasant, leafy glade. The grass is soft beneath my feet and the light is dappled as the sunshine filters through the leaves of the trees. It is a warm day and there is a gentle breeze blowing.

I walk along the grassy path, looking at the flowers and trees as I pass, admiring their colours and perfumes. I can hear the birds singing around me and their song lifts my spirits and helps me to feel happy to be alive and to be in this beautiful place.

Now I have come to a clearing and I can feel the sun's rays warming the whole of my body. As the warmth penetrates my skin, my muscles relax and all tension disappears. I close my eyes and imagine that the rays of the sun are a warm shower flowing over the outside of my body and also flowing within me, from my head to my toes. I visualize this shower of golden sunlight passing slowly from my head, down my neck, across my shoulders and then all the way down inside my body and my limbs. When it reaches the place where I have been experiencing pain, it washes that pain away and carries it down my body until it slips away through my fingers or my toes.

I am aware that I feel warmed and cleansed by this shower of sunlight, both on the outside and on the inside. I am aware that I am now fully relaxed and free of pain. I shall stay in the sunshine for as long as I wish. When I eventually open my eyes, my body will be so relaxed and so cleansed that the pain will have disappeared.

Suggested affirmations

• My pain has been washed away
• My body is relaxed and I feel no pain.

SURGERY

There may be times when surgery is necessary – and here too Life Scripts can make a great deal of difference to the speed and effectiveness of your recovery. Indeed, in the past few years several of the main teaching hospitals have been using cassettes of positive suggestions during and immediately after surgery and they have found that such techniques do in fact help the patient's recovery.

Hypnotherapists have realized for some time that an anaesthetized patient can still hear – although obviously on a different level. When regressed to times of surgery, such patients have been able to repeat conversations heard in the operating theatre itself – and it is for this reason that many theatre staff have now been cautioned to be careful what they say at such times.

There are two scripts in this section; one is to be used before the surgery takes place (although naturally this is not possible in the case of an accident or emergency) while the other is for the post-operative period. You can begin to use the latter as soon as your head has cleared sufficiently for you to concentrate on what you are doing. Even better is if you can have someone else read the script to you as soon as (or even before) you wake from the anaesthetic. You may not be intellectually aware of what is being said but your subconscious will still hear and accept the words.

Surgery script – 1

I am aware that I am in a state of relaxation, both physically and mentally, and I know that at this present time it is very important for me to be as free from tension as possible and to practise the relaxation technique frequently.

Although no one can truly say that they are looking forward to undergoing surgery, nonetheless there is pleasure and relief in the thought that it will put an end to the condition which has made it necessary. By the time I leave hospital and return home, I will be on the way to a complete recovery without the pain or discomfort which has been with me so far.

I know that, by using my mind, I can speed up my body's natural healing process. I can begin now, even before I go into hospital, by preparing myself mentally, physically and emotionally for what is to come.

Unless I have been given a specific diet to follow – in which case, of course, I will do what is asked of me – I can ensure that I am as strong as possible by making certain that I eat a balanced diet and one which provides me with all the vitamins and minerals necessary for a healthy body. If there is a particular type of food I find unpalatable, I can take the vitamins or minerals it would provide in supplement form. This is one area of my health where I am in complete control.

I will use visualization to imagine myself as I shall be when I have returned to complete strength and fitness after the operation. I see myself moving and acting as I do when perfectly well and free from any pain and discomfort. I know that, by using visualization in this way, my mind will work towards making those images reality and that I shall recover more quickly than I otherwise would.

Every day I shall practise the relaxation technique and I shall increase its power by adding the word 'health' to it. While I am relaxing, I shall concentrate on the slow and steady rhythm of my breathing and, every time I exhale, I shall think the word 'health' to myself. My subconscious will be aware of this word and, every time I think it, that awareness of it will deepen. When the time comes for me to be in hospital, and right up until the time for the anaesthetic, I shall continue to relax and think the word 'health'. It will be the last thought in my mind before I drift into the anaesthetized state.

I shall stay here now in the depths of this wonderful relaxation, thinking the word 'health' as I exhale, until I feel like opening my eyes.

Use this script as often as you can before the time comes to go into hospital. Take it with you, in cassette form, to play in the run-up to surgery itself.

Suggested affirmations

- I can control what I eat and my vitamin intake
- Soon I shall be free of pain and discomfort
- Health.

Surgery script – 2

The surgery is over and I can now concentrate on becoming strong and well again. I know that, by using the power of my mind, I can make this happen very quickly.

As I relax, I imagine my natural life force circulating throughout my body. I visualize it as a colour and concentrate on *seeing* that colour spreading from the top of my head down through my body and my limbs until it is everywhere within me. The energy of my natural life force will speed up my body's own healing ability and I know that I shall very soon be feeling fit and well and free from whatever pain or discomfort has been troubling me.

I also visualize the scar left by the surgery and I imagine it growing smaller and fainter as I see it. Because the mind can control so many of the body's processes, I know that the scar will soon be no more than a pale shadow of what it is now.

Each time I relax and breathe slowly and evenly, I think the word 'health' to myself as I exhale. I know that, by doing this, I am reinforcing in my subconscious mind the concept of a return to complete health.

I take great pleasure in the thought that I shall soon be fit and well again and that I shall have played a part in my own speedy recovery.

I shall stay in this relaxed state for as long as I wish, breathing slowly and concentrating on the word 'health' each time that I exhale.

Suggested affirmations

- My natural life force will speed up the healing process
- I shall make a quick and complete recovery
- Health.

PANIC ATTACKS

Panic (or anxiety) attacks may arise for a variety of reasons but the truth is often hidden somewhere in the past. If you suffer from them regularly or frequently, you really need to seek professional help from an appropriate therapist or counsellor who will help you determine their cause. However, the Life Script given here will enable you to deal with the symptoms on a temporary basis when the panic arises. It is not intended as a substitute for unearthing the cause – but in the meantime it is certainly better for you than becoming reliant on tablets.

Until the cause has been unearthed, you may still experience the onset of sensations of panic. The important thing is to use the script at the first possible opportunity. Once you are in the middle of a full-blown attack, you are not going to think calmly or logically enough to do so. So, whatever you are doing, stop for a few moments and concentrate on the script which follows. You will see that it involves concentration on breathing deeply. This is because, when in a state of panic, the tendency is to breathe solely from the upper chest area. This causes less oxygen to reach the brain and creates the light-headed or dizzy sensation so often associated with panic. As always, the script should follow the relaxation technique already given.

Panic attacks script

I have relaxed my body as much as possible and I am going to spend just a few moments eliminating all sense of panic or anxiety from my mind and my body.

I visualize the panic as a black and murky substance which fills my whole being. I am going to find a way to replace that blackness with the pure white of peace and strength.

I begin by breathing as deeply as I can, imagining that with each breath I inhale pure white light. As I breathe out, I exhale some of this murky substance which has been circulating within me. I shall continue to do this for several moments, breathing a little more deeply as soon as I can – always seeing the air I breathe in as pure and white while the air I breathe out is thick and black.

As the white light mingles with the blackness inside me, the air I exhale becomes a dark grey rather than black. I continue to breathe even more deeply and, as I do, the air I exhale becomes lighter in colour until it is a mid-grey and then a light grey.

Now I am breathing very deeply indeed and all the foul blackness has been expelled from my body. I am aware that the air I breathe out is now as pure and white as the air I breathe in. I am also aware that all sense of panic has disappeared.

Suggested affirmations

• I breathe in pure white light
• By breathing deeply I can dispel all sense of panic.

ASTHMA

It is not possible to cure asthma completely by means of Life Scripts – but it is certainly possible to ensure that attacks are far less frequent and that those which do appear are of minimal severity. Whatever its original cause, whether genetic or acquired, asthma is always exacerbated by tension or stress, particularly in those who are unable to find an outlet for that tension.

Asthma is also very frightening for the sufferer. The tightness in the chest and the sensation of being unable to breathe induce their own feelings of panic. This in turn increases the stress and therefore the severity of the attack. And so the poor asthmatic is often trapped in a vicious circle for which inhalants would seem to be the only means of acquiring temporary relief.

Over the years I have been practising hypnotherapy I have treated many, many asthmatics and I can assure you that in every case relief has been gained – and some (although still officially diagnosed as being asthmatic) have not had an attack for years.

The script given is designed to be used as soon as you have the first indication that an attack might be imminent. Think about what usually happens. The moment you get that 'early-warning signal', you begin to get anxious. 'Oh, no. Please don't let it happen.' You grow frightened; this causes physical tension which of course makes it more difficult to breathe. The attack appears to grow in intensity and you panic even more. Before you know it, you are in the midst of a full-blown asthma attack, gasping for breath and feeling dreadful.

There is no point waiting for such an attack before trying to use a Life Script. For one thing you will have set up such a train of physical reactions that it would be very difficult to practise the exercise given and, for another, you will not be thinking clearly enough even to set it in motion. So, when you have that first indication that an attack might be imminent, instead of thinking 'Oh, no', think 'Life Script' and you will be able to disperse the attack before it even begins. You will be in control.

For many people, the knowledge that they can exercise this amount of control and need never suffer a full-blown asthma attack again is enough to help them to feel sufficiently at peace for the attacks to disappear altogether. But, even if you are not this lucky, you could cope perfectly well if you never had more than an occasional warning signal.

Asthma script

My body is as relaxed as I can make it and my mind is at peace because I know that I can dispel this threatening bout of asthma before it manages to have any noticeable effect on me.

As I sit here, I conjure up a scene in my mind. I am walking along a grassy lane. It is a beautiful day, warm and sunny, but not too hot, and there is a gentle breeze blowing. I walk at a leisurely pace, taking the time to look around me at the grass, the trees and the flowers. With every step that I take, I breathe more easily and more deeply, enjoying the scents of nature.

This path is unfamiliar to me so I am curious to discover where it will lead. It passes along between some old trees which cast a cool, green shadow and then I find myself out in the sunlight once more and I realize that I am walking along a grassy cliff top, always keeping a safe distance from the edge of the cliff itself. I can smell the sea now and I turn and look down to my right. Below me is a deserted beach of soft, white sand beyond which I can see the sea itself – a brilliant blue on such a lovely day. The wavelets make a gentle, rippling sound as they reach out to touch the shore.

I turn now to look out over the bay. The scent of the sea is carried towards me by the breeze and I breathe slowly and deeply, allowing it to fill my lungs. With every breath I take, my body relaxes more and more and my mind is more and more at peace. I feel healthy and strong.

The sea air makes me feel drowsy, so I lie down on the soft grass of the clifftop and close my eyes. I can feel the warmth of the sun on my body and the gentle touch of the breeze on my skin. I can hear the rhythmic melody of the waves on the shore and even the sound of seabirds calling. As I lie here I continue to breathe deeply and evenly, allowing the sea-scented air to fill my whole being.

I shall lie amid the sounds and scents of this beautiful place for as long as I wish. When I am completely free from all tension, I shall quietly open my eyes.

When you first begin to use this script to help you prevent an asthma attack, you will probably need to work through the whole thing from beginning to end. However, once you are used to it and have proved to yourself how well it works, you may reach the stage where all you have to do is to picture the scene and you will immediately begin to breathe deeply from your diaphragm, thus releasing the tension from your body.

Suggested affirmations

- If I picture the sea I can breathe deeply and easily
- I can release the tension from my body
- I control my asthma; it cannot control me.

MIGRAINE

There are two main types of migraine attack. One is brought about by an allergic reaction to something eaten or drunk. The most common culprits are cheese, red wine and chocolate so, if you know that these affect you, I'm afraid you'll just have to give them up. The second – and far more common – form of migraine is brought about by excess stress and tension and this is the one you can learn to control.

Although what I am referring to here is a full-blown migraine attack with its accompanying symptoms of eye pain and nausea as opposed to a severe headache, the script given will work perfectly well for the latter too. As with the script for controlling asthma, the time to use it is when you have the very first indications that an attack is approaching. Most people are well able to recognize this moment but the most common – and quite understandable – reaction is to be so filled with anxiety or dread that you immediately become even more tense and thereby increase the likelihood of the migraine taking hold. If you could be absolutely certain that you could turn that feeling around whenever you wanted to and make the migraine disappear before it became any stronger, you would avoid all that excessive tension.

The main area of difficulty arises if you happen to be one of those sufferers who wakes up in the morning to find that you are already in the midst of a migraine attack. Since it will already have taken hold, presumably the early warning signs – if there were any – would have presented themselves while you were asleep and unable to do anything constructive about it. If this applies to you, try using the script in bed at night before going to sleep.

This ensures that your sleep will be relaxed when perhaps it might otherwise not be. If you are completely relaxed, you cannot suffer a migraine attack, so it is unlikely that you will wake to find one has already arrived.

As always, this script should be preceded by the relaxation technique you have already practised.

Migraine script

I am aware that my body is completely relaxed as I imagine myself lying on the most comfortable bed in existence in a lovely room. This room is decorated in muted shades of my favourite colours and the atmosphere is one of peace and tranquillity. There are no sounds other than my own rhythmic breathing.

As I lie there, an invisible hand places a cube of pink ice in the centre of my forehead. Immediately there is a cool sensation which spreads over the whole of my forehead. As this pink ice cube comes into contact with the warmth of my skin it begins to melt – but very slowly. I can feel the cool pink water beginning to trickle down from the centre of my forehead to my temples.

Now the pink ice melts a little more and the cool water slowly glides down to the area around my eyes and to my eyelids themselves, reducing the temperature and leaving me feeling clear-headed and refreshed.

As the ice melts even more, the pink water from my temples flows down the sides of my face to the pulse points behind my ears and from there down my neck to the pulse point at my throat.

The ice has now completely melted and my head feels cool and refreshed. I know that when I open my eyes they will be bright and clear – just as my thought processes will be clear and untroubled.

I lie here on this comfortable bed in the beautiful room I have created in my imagination. I concentrate on the steady rhythm of my breathing and on the wonderful sense of clarity and alertness I feel. I shall stay like this for as long as I wish, knowing that when I open my eyes I shall be perfectly well and able to do whatever I want.

Suggested affirmations

• Pink ice will cool and clear my head
• I need never suffer from migraine again.

INSOMNIA

Insomnia brings many miseries, whether you are one of those people who finds it impossible to get to sleep in the first place or whether you fall asleep easily enough only to wake during the night.

The Life Script which follows will help you in either case. You can use it both to go to sleep when you first go to bed and to go back to sleep after you have woken. (What usually happens in the latter case, of course, is that you lie there growing more annoyed with yourself, watching the clock and calculating how few hours you have left if you want to get a decent night's sleep.)

Before using the script, however, there are several things you can do to help create the right atmosphere for sleep.

• Try to establish a pre-bed routine. You might like to have a warm drink, read a magazine, take a leisurely bath or brush your hair. Whatever it is, if you do it regularly, it is rather like preparing your subconscious for the fact that it is time for sleep.

• Avoid anything too stimulating just before going to bed. Don't attempt to work right up to the last moment or drink coffee or alcohol (a drink might help you go to sleep but you'll soon wake up again).

• If you are someone who lies there thinking of things

which need to be done and you're worried you might not remember them, keep a pad and pencil by your bed. That way, if you are struck by a vital thought during the night, you can jot it down and then go back to sleep, secure in the knowledge that you cannot possibly forget it.

Insomnia script

I am lying in my bed, completely relaxed and happy in the knowledge that, with the aid of this script, I can drift easily to sleep and that the sleep itself will be deep and refreshing. If I should happen to wake during the night, I shall simply repeat the script and I will soon go back to sleep again.

In my imagination I create a beautiful garden. It can be one with which I am familiar or I can simply invent one. I am walking around that garden early on a sunny afternoon. The sun is high overhead in a brilliant blue sky. All the colours around me are strong and vibrant – the red and gold hues of summer flowers, the bright green of the grass, the clear blue of the sky. It is a happy garden and I can hear the birds singing and the bees humming as scarlet butterflies flit from bush to bush.

Now I am standing in that same garden but it is late afternoon so the colours are more muted. Trees cast long fingers of shadow across the grass and the flowers look less brilliant in this gentler light – indeed some of them have even begun to fold their petals ready for the night. The air is still warm and heavy with perfume but the strong heat of the day has faded. I stand still, absorbing the peace and calm of the garden.

It is night-time and I have decided to take a stroll around my beautiful garden. Everything is shadow now but the sky appears pale by contrast and I can see the trees and bushes in silhouette. The colours of the flowers have faded with the fading light although their perfume still fills the air. Here and there I can make out a few white blossoms in the darkness. All is silent; the birds and the bees are asleep. There is a wonderful sense of peace in my garden and I shall stay here, on this warm summer night, for as long as I wish.

The most likely result of using this script is that you will fall into a deep and relaxed sleep. But even if you do not, you will slow your heart and pulse rate, relax your body and reduce your blood-pressure rather as an animal does when it hibernates. If this is the only thing you are able to achieve, you will still be able to get up in the morning feeling alert and refreshed.

Suggested affirmations

• When I relax, sleep will come to me
• I can sleep whenever I wish
• I will always wake feeling refreshed.

PMT

Pre-menstrual tension is a miserable condition bringing with it a variety of possible problems, ranging from physical discomfort to headaches, tearfulness, irritability and even irrational behaviour. Some women will suffer from just one or two symptoms while others seem to be tormented by many at the same time.

The first thing you should do, if you are a PMT sufferer, is to have a physical check-up by your own doctor or at a Well Woman Clinic. If, as happens in many cases, no specific reason is found for the PMT symptoms, then the Life Script given here should prove helpful. Even if some medical problem is diagnosed and treatment offered, the script which follows will still be beneficial.

There is a great deal of stress in many people's lives right now and this is particularly true of women – who have all the problems that men have plus some of their own. Even in relationships where her partner is sensitive and cooperative, it is usually the woman who assumes the bulk of the responsibility for caring for the home and the family – even if she has a demanding full-time career. For those women who travel on business, there is the added strain of staying alone in hotels or walking to your car at night. We can add to this, of course, the physical symptoms which may accompany menstruation, pregnancy or menopause.

One of the physical reactions caused by excess stress is the production of extra adrenalin. While this can be marvellous if you are just about to clinch that deal or make that presentation, an extra surge of adrenalin automatically reduces the production of the female hormones. This in turn contributes greatly to the PMT symptoms already described. These symptoms create even more stress in the sufferer and so the vicious circle is perpetuated.

It is also a fact that any muscle which is tensed – and when you are stressed your muscles automatically become tense – will experience more pain than a muscle which is relaxed. So PMT causes stress . . . which causes tension . . . which causes pain . . . which causes more stress . . . and so on.

To break this cycle of misery, try using the Life Script given below. You will have to use your own judgement about the ideal time to start working with it by thinking about your own monthly cycle and the time when you usually begin to experience the symptoms of PMT. For some women this will be anything up to a week before the start of a period; for others it will only be a day or so beforehand. Ideally you should start using the script about two days before the symptoms normally present themselves. In most cases, the symptoms reduce once the period has started but, if this does not apply to you, continue working with the script until you are sure the normal PMT time has passed. (This script should be used when lying down and after the normal relaxation technique.)

PMT script

As I relax, I imagine myself walking along a softly carpeted floor towards a white door. I open the door and enter the most beautiful and luxurious bathroom I have ever seen. It is furnished and decorated in the way which most appeals to me. There are plants around and thick carpet on the floor. In the centre of this room is a large bath filled with warm water which has been scented with my favourite perfume. I take off my clothes and step into this bath, sinking down into the water and feeling its warmth relax every muscle in my body. There is gentle music playing in the background and I lie in the scented bath, relaxing and thinking of nothing other than how good it feels to be here.

When I feel I have spent as long as I wish in the bath, I step out, wrapping myself in one of the huge, fluffy towels which are to hand. I choose from the many bottles containing oils and creams and stroke the one I select all over my body, letting it soften and perfume my skin. Now I slip into a lovely silken robe and make my way across the bathroom and through another white door.

I find myself now in a delightful bedroom which is also decorated and furnished as I would choose. There is a huge bed surrounded by beautiful drapes and linens and covered with a soft downy duvet. I lie on the bed, my head on the pillows, and I pull the duvet over me. I am still warm from the bath, my skin is smooth and perfumed and the duvet maintains that warmth so that my body and my mind relax more and more. I shall stay here in this bed until I feel that I would like to open my eyes.

Suggested affirmations

- Relaxation reduces PMT
- I am free from PMT
- I am in control of my own body.

6

Fulfilling Your Potential

Most people have the potential to achieve far more than they ever do. Perhaps this is because they doubt their own ability, feel that success is for 'other people' or are so lacking in self-confidence that they hesitate even to take the first step. Here, too, Life Scripts can help. By using them you can improve your learning ability, develop your creativity, become more positive and achieve more in specific situations, whether we are talking about taking exams or participating in sports.

DEVELOPING YOUR CREATIVITY

The brain has two halves – the left and the right. The left brain governs our logical thoughts (such as mathematics and analysis), while the right brain governs the creative side of our nature (such as imagination and artistic ability). Upbringing in most cases tends to favour left-brain activity so that, although little children have the most marvellous power of imagination, as we grow up many of us lose a great deal of this power. Naturally it is important to be able to analyse and to think logically – but it is just as important to be creative and imaginative too. Indeed, the successful use of Life Scripts depends to some extent on your ability to visualize and to make full use of your imagination. If you have found this unnatural in the early stages, please don't despair. Think of your imagination as a muscle. Like any other muscle in your body it can become weak if not used. But, like any other muscle, regular exercise can help increase its strength – possibly to limits never even considered before.

The very first Life Script given – the one to aid basic relaxation – will help to re-kindle your powers of imagination. And, since this script is an essential preliminary to any other you may be using, you will use it often enough to stretch your right-brain abilities and thus help yourself when it comes to fulfilling your creative potential.

If you wish to take creative development still further, another script is given below which will help you. It is based on a form of meditation which is easily accessible to everyone and should be used when you are looking for inspiration – whether to draw, paint, write or make use of any other of your creative talents. It will not make you a genius in your chosen field and it certainly cannot take the place of a basic knowledge of the skill you wish to develop. But it can ensure that you get maximum enjoyment from what you do and that the results are likely to be better than any you have previously achieved.

Creativity script

I am calm and relaxed and I am happy because I know that I am working towards enhancing my own creative powers in the way I choose. By using this script and the affirmations which accompany it, I shall become more inspired in the way that I paint (write) (sculpt) (think). I am beginning an ongoing process which will bring me joy and fulfilment in my creative life.

Using my powers of imagination, I picture myself standing in a room, facing a door which I know leads to the outside. I look at the door, noting the way it is made, the type of handle, lock and hinges it bears. Now I put my hand on the handle, pull open the door and make my way outside.

I find myself standing on a path which twists and turns into the distance as it meanders through the garden to a gate which I know is there but which is at present out of sight. I start to walk along the path, not hurrying but taking the time to look to the right and the left, taking in the scenery which my mind is creating.

Eventually the gate is in sight and I make my way towards it at a leisurely pace, enjoying the journey as much as the anticipation of arrival. As I approach the gate, I take the time to notice how it is made, of what material, how it opens and whether it is set in a wall, a fence or a hedge.

By the time I reach the gate, I am beginning to feel excited. I know that I am soon to learn something about the creative direction I will take in the future. I place my hand on the gate, feeling its texture; now I open it and pass through, closing the gate behind me.

(*At this point, allow your imagination to take over. Let your walk take you wherever your imagination decrees; don't try to influence it in any way – just allow yourself to drift along as the images unfold*)

I am enjoying the walk and the sights and sounds which surround me. I know that I can continue this journey into the special places created by my imagination for as long as I wish. As soon as I feel that I would like to return to the reality of the place I started from, I simply take two or three deep breaths and open my eyes.

Suggested affirmations

- My imagination is limitless
- I can become the creative person I have always wanted to be
- My right brain is developing daily.

LEARNING AND MEMORY

The more you develop your imagination and the more creative you become as an individual, the easier you will find it to absorb new knowledge. This applies whether we are talking about life experience or formal learning of a particular subject for a specific reason.

Just as we are brought up to be left-brained and logical in our attitude, our approach to learning also tends to be analytical and precise rather than creative. We try to absorb knowledge verbally rather than visually. Yet think of a small child, unable to speak or understand language; think how much that child learns of the world around him in a very short space of time. His learning has to be visual as he has not yet developed his verbal talents. If we could learn as the child does, by working with the pictures in our minds, combining this with the logical practical aspects of acquiring knowledge, how much more effective would we find the process and how much more information would we be able to absorb.

What do we usually do when we want to learn a language? We sit down with a text book and find ourselves confronted with lists of cases, clauses and irregular verbs. What does a child do when learning to speak his language? He starts with a simple word linked to an object which he recognizes visually and builds up from there. 'Ball,' he will say; then 'want ball' and a little later, 'me want ball'. No declensions or conjugations for him. If you want to learn another language, start with a toy, perhaps a doll's house with rooms and furniture or a toy garage with petrol pumps and cars. Label each item with its name in your chosen language – and play with them. If you've really forgotten how to play, find a child to share the game with you and you can both learn at the same time.

There may be many reasons why you might want to improve your learning ability. Perhaps you are a student, whether young or mature; you may be working towards a promotion, or be in a career where new documentation is frequently presented to you; you might need to study the Highway Code; or you may just enjoy learning new things for their own sake. Whatever the reason, the Life Scripts which follow can help you. Naturally, because there are so many possible reasons for using them, they have had to be couched in fairly general terms. But don't let this prevent you from adding specific words and phrases or altering them in order to fit your particular set of circumstances. In fact, with these, as with all the Life Scripts in this book, the more you are able to personalize the script, the more effective you will find it. (At the end of the first script you will find some suggestions for adapting facts into visual images.) As always, it should be preceded by the relaxation technique.

Improving learning ability script – 1

I am completely relaxed in mind and body and I am ready to begin using my own creative powers to increase and enhance my learning ability. This is how, as a small child, I learned about the world around me; I did so effortlessly and in a way which was natural to me. I am about to rediscover the natural way to acquire, absorb and retain knowledge and information by using my right-brain abilities. I have the added advantage that I have also discovered over the years how to use my left-brain abilities and so, by combining and balancing the two, the way in which I learn will be further improved.

As soon as I have finished using this script, I am going to look in the book which contains the facts I wish to absorb. I realize that, in order to make the book easy to read, the author has had to place those facts into sentences or phrases. I have no need to remember every word of such sentences – only the actual facts they surround. Each page of text is unlikely to carry more than ten or twelve actual facts – I shall think of these as Key Facts.

As I look at each page of the book, I shall make a list of the Key Facts to be found on it. The number of pages I feel able to work on during any one session will depend on the complexity of the text and I accept that there is no point in forcing myself to attempt more than I am capable of doing in a single session.

Once I have extracted the Key Facts, I shall convert each one into an image which I can retain as a picture in my mind. The more amusing or original I can make that image the easier it will be to remember. I am aware that everyone finds it simpler to recall the odd or the unusual than the mundane. And, because I have already worked on developing my creative self, I shall soon become adept at inventing memorable images for my Key Facts.

I shall relax for a few moments more and then, when I feel ready, I shall open my eyes.

Suggested affirmations

- Think 'pictures'
- Learn like a child
- Key facts matter.

Here are a few suggestions for images which might be relevant in different learning situations. You may choose to use them as written – or you may allow your creative self to take over and invent others for yourself.

History

Invent a mental 'photograph' of the character mentioned. It doesn't matter if you don't really know what Joan of Arc, Henry II or Vasco da Gama really looked like – make it up! Then you will be able to 'see' your character performing the actions you need to learn.

Highway Code

Take, for example, the chart of stopping distances – never easy to learn in the normally accepted way. Visualize the vehicle braking suddenly and then someone (perhaps a favourite cartoon character) leaping out and using a tape measure to calculate the distance between your car and the one in front.

Foreign language

Visualize a scene where every item and every person has a large label attached bearing the word which applies to them. (If you want to make this even easier to remember, stick the labels in unusual places!)

Mathematics

Either personify the numbers by giving them faces (people you know?), arms and legs and let them move about or use the label system. For example, the square root of 81 is 9. (I know that's very basic – but so is my maths!) Perhaps you could imagine a plant in a pot, the label bearing the number 81. The pot is transparent and you can see the roots (square of course) reaching down into the earth; at the end of the longest root is a ticket with the number 9.

Improving learning ability script – 2

My body and my mind are relaxed and I have worked at developing my creative self. Now I am ready to use my newly-enhanced powers to help me remember the Key Facts I have selected and for which I have chosen appropriate images.

From the Key Facts taken from the page(s) I have been reading, I shall create a moving picture in my imagination. The objects or characters I have imagined will form part of this moving picture and they will act and react in a sequence which helps to fix the images in my mind.

(*At this point allow the scene you have chosen to play in your imagination for as long as is necessary.*)

Those images – and the Key Facts they represent – are now firmly fixed in my mind and my memory. I shall be able to recall them at will.

Suggested affirmations

- I can see the pictures in my mind
- Images make me learn and remember.

Using mental pictures, whether still or moving, is a highly effective method of committing anything to memory – from someone's name to a shopping list. Remember that the more amusing, or even ridiculous, you can make the image, the easier it will be to remember. If a man's name is Henry, you might have trouble remembering the picture of him carrying a hen – but you will have no difficulty recalling his name if your image is of the man with a big, brown hen sitting on his head.

SPECIFIC SITUATIONS

In addition to ongoing problems, there are many one-off situations we have to face which can cause a great deal of apprehension. Here, too, an appropriate Life Script can prove invaluable. The types of situation I have in mind are:

- Going for an interview
- Taking an examination
- Making a speech or a report
- Taking a driving test

- Chairing a meeting for the first time
- Giving a performance.

A similar technique is used for the above or any similar situation so, rather than give a separate script for each one, I have chosen the first – going for an interview. If the situation you have to deal with is one of the others, you should have no difficulty in adapting the script accordingly.

Going for an interview script

I am feeling warm, comfortable and relaxed as I contemplate the interview which will soon take place. Although it is important to me, I know that I will only acquit myself well if I am both well prepared and as much at ease as I can be.

To this end I am going to rehearse the entire interview in my mind, very much as an actor rehearses his part in a play when he wishes to give a perfect performance. Before I do so, I shall always take the time to relax, to breathe slowly and regularly, and to feel comfortable.

I imagine myself standing outside the door of the interview room. It does not matter if I have never been to that room before; one office is much like another. It does not matter if I do not even know whether the person who will be interviewing me will be male or female; I can make it whichever I like in my mind as it is *my* performance and *my* reactions which are important.

Before entering the room, I make sure that my shoulders and neck are as free from tension as I can make them. I relax my jaw and take a couple of deep breaths. I enter the room to be greeted by the interviewer who asks me to sit. I sit down, making sure that I am comfortable and that my posture is upright but not rigid. I do not fold my arms across my body but see myself leaning slightly forwards, a slight smile on my lips as the interviewer begins to ask me questions.

Logic will let me know the type of questions I am likely to be asked and, with this in mind, I allow the whole scene to play through in my imagination – seeing myself acting exactly as I would wish to do, appearing calm and confident. Every now and then, during this visualization, I pause to reassure myself that I am still feeling relaxed and my breathing is still steady.

As my pictured interview comes to an end, I rise from my seat, shake hands with the interviewer and leave the room. I know that I have done everything perfectly.

The more detail you are able to build in to your imagined scene the better. So, if possible, decide in advance what you are going to wear; this will enable you to be wearing that particular outfit when using the script. You know what is on your own CV and also what the company's business is. You will therefore be able to work out in advance what some of the questions are likely to be and build your responses into the scene as you imagine it.

Using the Life Script to prepare for an interview will not guarantee that you are offered the position you seek; it may be that someone else comes along who is far better qualified. What it will do is ensure that you do everything perfectly so that you have no reason to reproach yourself afterwards. This in turn increases your confidence when contemplating future interviews.

Suggested affirmations

- Like the actor, I must rehearse if I am to give a perfect performance
- The interview will be a complete personal success.

IMPROVING SPORTING PERFORMANCE

Just as acting perfectly at an interview may not guarantee that you will be offered a specific job, using Life Scripts to improve your sporting performance cannot make you a winner if you do not have as much strength or skill as someone else. But it will ensure that you give the best performance possible.

Life Scripts are no substitute for knowledge and experience. Visualizing yourself hitting a hole in one will not work if you have never learned how to handle a golf club. Nor will you win the 100 metres sprint if you have not exercised and trained. However, provided you have the initial training and skill required, you will certainly improve your performance considerably.

You will note, during the course of the script, that you are being asked to recall a previous success. Don't make the mistake of thinking this has to be a success in the relevant sport you are now working on. You don't even have had to win a prize or a trophy. Perhaps 'success' was yours on the day you first managed to swim a width, bake a perfect sponge cake or gain a cub scout badge. What matters is the way you *felt* at that moment, however great or small the success may have been. Pause for a moment right now and decide on a successful moment in your past; it might have been twenty years ago or it might have been yesterday. When you have found it, you are ready to go on to the script below.

Improving sporting performance script

As I relax here, listening to the slow and steady rhythm of my breathing, I picture the moment I have already selected as a moment when I experienced success. I remember it in as much detail as possible but I remember particularly how I felt at the time. At that moment I knew what it was to achieve and to be proud of myself.

As I remember that moment, I think of the first word connected with it to come into my mind. By recalling that word at will, I will be able to fix that feeling of success and achievement forever in my subconscious mind. So that the word is etched firmly in my subconscious, I imagine it being written in block capitals, one letter at a time, in white chalk on a blackboard. I do this three times.

Now I turn to the sport in which I wish to excel. In as much detail as possible, I imagine myself taking part in that sport. Because I know that using all the senses makes such imagery even more powerful, I do not simply *see* what I am doing – I *feel* (the racquet in my hand) (the water I am swimming in), I *hear* (the sound of ball hitting bat) (the sound of the wind), and I *smell* (the freshly cut grass) (the salt sea water). Using all these senses, I observe myself going through all the actions necessary for the sport in question and doing everything perfectly.

At the same time, I repeat to myself, silently or aloud, the word I intuitively selected to remind me of my earlier success.

Each time I use this script my subconscious mind will come to accept that there is a natural link between my sporting ability and the sensation of success, and my prowess will increase more than I could have believed possible.

Suggested affirmations

- (*Insert your chosen word*)
- I have been a success before and I shall be a success again
- My mind and my body are working together to improve my sport.

7

Pregnancy and Childbirth

Even when a pregnancy has been planned and wanted, there are occasions when it may not be the joyous and positive experience it should be. No matter how many books she reads or people she talks to, the first-time mother is bound to feel anxious about the pregnancy itself, about the experience of childbirth and about how she will cope with caring for her baby once it has been born. Indeed, it is often the case that the more she reads and the more she hears of other people's experiences, the *more* anxious she becomes.

For some women, the road to conception has been long and difficult and the tension this will have created in her may cause her to be in a less positive state of mind during her pregnancy than she would wish.

There are also those who have suffered the tragedy of a miscarriage and who will therefore be even more anxious during an ensuing pregnancy. Even when everything appears to be going well, a part of them will be frightened to look forward in case something similar happens again. It does not help in such cases to be told that 'it happens to many women' or that 'it does not necessarily affect future pregnancies'. A miscarriage is such a traumatic event that the woman may well appear uncaring or diffident about her new pregnancy when all she is in fact doing is providing herself with an emotional suit of armour to protect her against possible distress.

The matter is not made any easier by the lack of understanding of how the mother is feeling which still exists today. I have had many patients who have been through the trauma of a miscarriage and they tell me that in many areas there is still a total lack of counselling. Because they usually return to physical health fairly quickly, it is assumed that they will 'get over it' with equal speed. One young woman told me that her sister, who had given birth to a healthy child, was being seen at a local mother and baby clinic and by a health visitor who called at her home whereas she, who had lost her baby in the fifth month of pregnancy, was left to cope alone. For many women the greatest help and strength is to be found from contact with others at their local branch of the Miscarriage Association (of which further details can be found in the final section of this book).

Should you have the misfortune to suffer a miscarriage, it is important that you go through all the grieving processes as described in the section on bereavement. In fact, the Life Script on dealing with bereavement can help both father and mother to come to terms with their loss. Ideally you should go through this process before conceiving again. It will not remove all fears but it will help you to look forwards in a more positive and optimistic way.

CONCEPTION

For some couples, conception is uncomplicated, whereas for others it may be a long and traumatic process. The more desperately you long for a baby and the harder you try, the more conception seems to evade you. (I am not dealing here with couples who suffer from an actual physical condition making conception difficult, but with the many who have been told by their doctor that there is no reason why they should not have a child – and yet nothing seems to happen.) In particular the woman who feels she is getting towards the end of her childbearing years may become so tense that the longed-for pregnancy never seems to happen.

An excellent organization exists called Foresight (details later) which gives advice on physical and emotional pre-conceptual care for both mother and father. This applies not only to couples experiencing difficulty in conceiving, but any future parents who wish to give their child the best possible start in life.

Problems related to conception do nothing to enhance the relationship between the man and woman. They may begin to feel that the formerly joyful process of making love has become so regulated by the taking of temperatures and the calculation of optimum ovulation times that all spontaneity has departed. The woman is not helped by being told to 'relax' during the sexual act. If the only thing on her mind is that, if she fails to conceive within the next few days, she will probably have to wait another whole month, she is not going to find it easy to comply. It is, however, true that if she *can* be more relaxed then she is more likely to become pregnant – so what is she to do?

The difficulty is that it is impossible to stop thinking something just because you have been told to. Try this: think of an elephant. Go on – do it now. Really *see* that elephant in your imagination – its long trunk, thick hide, large ears and ivory tusks. Now, stop thinking of the elephant. You can't, can you?

But, if I were to ask you to make a list of everything you have eaten today and you started to think about that, you would stop thinking about the elephant! The point is that you can only bring one thought to an end by replacing it with another. So, instead of concentrating on trying to relax (which is an anachronism in itself), why not indulge in a few delicious fantasies while making love? Make the occasion something to look forward to for reasons other than physical satisfaction or the possibility of conception. Not only would you add a great deal of fun and spice to your love life but you would be far more relaxed in the process – and therefore the desired pregnancy is more likely to result.

I am not going to provide you with a script for your fantasy. I am sure you can think up something far better than I would ever write! But, whether you choose to imagine your favourite film star or fictional hero or whether you like to visualize exotic locations or unusual situations, make sure that you enjoy it.

Whether you have been trying hard to become pregnant or are simply looking forward to it, there is a Life Script which you will find beneficial. It has also proved useful for women undergoing such treatment as IVF who are obviously experiencing a considerable amount of tension – not only are they pinning all their hopes on the treatment but it is costing them a lot of money too. The script itself helps the woman prepare herself emotionally and, by using the subconscious, prepare herself physically too. (As always, it should be preceded by the basic relaxation technique.)

Conception script

I am feeling relaxed, warm and comfortable and I am going to use my mind and my imagination to prepare my body for the wonderful experience of pregnancy.

Just as a newborn baby needs loving and nurturing, so too does the tiny child in the womb. Because I know that my conscious and subconscious mind have a great effect upon the condition of my body, I am going to use them to create the softest and most loving place I can for the child I am going to conceive.

As I lie here, I place my hand gently over the lower part of my body so that it is directly above the area of my womb, the place where my child will grow and develop. If I concentrate, I can feel the warmth of my hand upon my skin and eventually that warmth penetrates the skin and spreads deep inside my body.

At the centre of that point of warmth, I visualize a tiny green shoot growing. In my imagination I watch that green shoot growing and developing until it turns into leaves and a stem. On top of the stem is a small pink bud. Slowly . . . very slowly . . . that bud swells and develops. Now, although it is still closed, I can make out the individual petals.

My breathing is very gentle and even and I am concentrating on the tiny pink bud. Slowly . . . very slowly . . . the petals are unfolding. Gradually the bud opens into a beautiful pink flower with soft, velvety petals. The outer petals are of a delicate, pale pink while the inner ones are a soft, deep rose in colour. Those inner petals curve slightly upwards and inwards forming a warm protected centre to the flower. That centre of the flower will provide a soft, safe place for my baby to rest and to grow.

As I relax, I visualize the opened flower filling the entire area of my womb and I know that, as the child within me grows, the petals of the flower will open wider still to accommodate the baby. The layers of petals will cushion and protect him until he is strong enough and big enough to be born.

I shall stay in this relaxed position, enjoying the sensation of creating this safe, loving place for my baby deep within my body. When I feel ready, I will quietly open my eyes and then remain in this position for several moments before rising.

This script should be used daily until such time as your pregnancy is confirmed. After that, it is a good idea to use it two or three times a week for the first three months, adapting it slightly to incorporate the image of a tiny baby cushioned in the centre of the flower.

Suggested affirmations

- My body is ready to receive and carry a baby
- The pink flower is safe and protective
- Love is soft and warm like the petals of a flower.

MOTHER/BABY LINKING

Even if they have not paid a great deal of attention to pre-conceptual care, most women, once their pregnancy has been confirmed, do whatever they can to care for the welfare of their unborn child. If they are sensible, they will watch their diet, take vitamin and mineral supplements, get plenty of rest, particularly in the later months, and certainly abstain from smoking. What many of them do not do is communicate with their baby.

From as early as the third or fourth month of the pregnancy, the baby is aware of the emotional atmosphere surrounding itself and its mother. This becomes obvious when you observe someone being hypnotically regressed to the womb. This is something I have done on many occasions as part of therapy and it is fascinating to note how sensitive the unborn child is to the moods of those closest to it. Although unable to recall actual words or situations, someone regressed in this way can certainly tell you whether their mother was happy, angry, frightened or sad. And, just as physical nutrition is passed from mother to baby, so too is the emotional state. Contented mother, contented baby; distressed mother, distressed baby.

If this is the case, surely it is vital for any pregnant woman who desires the best for her child to spend time communicating with that child, sending out thoughts of love and protection, even talking aloud so that the baby is aware of the sound of her voice.

Both mother and child benefit from this process. One of my patients who always became anxious when she had to attend the ante-natal clinic at the hospital found that by concentrating on reassuring the baby that everything was going to be all right, she managed to allay her own fears. After all, we do this with our children after they are born. Think of all the times you hear someone say, 'There, now. Everything is going to be all right. Mummy's here.' Why not comfort the baby within you in just the same way?

The Life Script which follows is designed to facilitate this mother/baby linking. It can be used from as early in the pregnancy as you wish but certainly from twelve weeks onwards. At first all you may wish to do is follow the script and send love to your child so that it feels safe and cherished. In the later stages, however, it is a good idea to talk to the baby, simply telling it about your day – what you have been doing, where you have been, and so on. The actual content of the conversation is relatively unimportant; it is the fact that the baby is becoming accustomed to your voice which matters. Because you will have practised the relaxation technique before beginning, the child will subconsciously link your voice and the sensation of love with a feeling of being at peace – and you will find that this creates a more contented newborn baby.

You might like to select a piece of music to play while using the following Life Script. I have been told by the expectant mothers I have worked with that if the same piece of music is used to accompany the relaxation session throughout the pregnancy, after the child is born it tends to react to that particular tune as if it were a lullaby. Naturally, since you are going to be listening to it for several months, it is advisable to choose something you are happy to hear over and over again. It can be modern or classical, middle-of-the-road or 'new age'. The type of music is unimportant, although you should select something which is melody only rather than a piece with words. You would find the words distracting, making concentration on the relaxation technique and the script more difficult.

To use this script, find a quiet time and place every day. Start the music, sit or lie comfortably, relax as best you can and then continue.

Mother/baby linking script

I am very relaxed, listening to the beautiful music playing gently in the background. I am very happy, looking forward with loving anticipation to seeing and holding my child. For the next few moments we are going to relax here together allowing the music to surround us.

As I think of you, my baby, I am aware of the warmth of a very deep love filling my entire being and, with all the power I possess, I send these thoughts of love to you. Let them surround you, allow yourself to be cocooned in the protective strength of my love. Know that there is not a moment in the day or night, whatever I may be doing and however my thoughts appear to be distracted, that I do not love you. I am holding you now, safely within my body. Before long I shall be holding you safely in my arms and sending you these same thoughts of love.

You are loved and you are cherished and, as the music surrounds us both, I want you to be aware of a sensation of peace and contentment. I know that, after you are born, this particular piece of music will always induce that sensation within you.

(*In the later months, it is at this point that you should speak aloud to the baby, telling it about your life, your family, the preparations you are making for its birth . . . and anything else you wish.*)

Let us now spend this precious time together, in feelings of love, peace and contentment, until the music ends.

Of course you can use this script as many times a day as you wish and for as long as you like on each occasion but I would suggest that you practise it at least once a day for about twenty minutes. (If you are using music which has been recorded on cassette, you can select a piece to last about that time.)

Suggested affirmations

- Whenever I think of my baby I feel a deep love
- I am surrounding my child with love and protection
- We are growing ever closer.

CHILDBIRTH

No two women will experience childbirth in precisely the same way. Indeed, there are many factors which may make a difference: the age, strength and general well-being of the mother; whether or not this is a first pregnancy; whether there have been any problems during the pregnancy; the choice of having the baby at home or in hospital . . . to name but a few. In addition, there are those women who insist upon a completely natural labour while others prefer to make use of whatever medication is offered to them. Some, of course, will find that they have no choice in the matter should a Caesarian section become necessary.

Whatever type of birth you experience, the Life Script which follows is designed to make you more relaxed and therefore less likely to experience pain. And if you are relaxed then your baby will be as relaxed as possible too, despite the fact that he will be undergoing what must be a traumatic experience.

You will notice in this particular script the words 'unless you are told otherwise by a doctor, nurse or midwife'. This is very important and should not be left out as no one can be sure at what speed events will happen or even when an emergency might arise. The script is designed to be as helpful as possible but the instructions of those caring for you professionally must always take precedence. So, whether this script is being read to you or whether you record it for yourself, *never* leave out those vital words.

Many hospitals now have cassette-playing equipment in delivery rooms but, in case it is faulty or there is none available, it is a good idea to take a personal portable cassette player with you. If you use one of the types which has headphones attached, the sound of the words of the script being spoken will help to concentrate your mind on what you are doing, and yet you will still hear and understand anyone who speaks directly to you.

Childbirth script

I am just about to take part in one of the most profound experiences of my life and I intend to do all that I can to make it a joyous time, both for me and for my baby.

At all times I will follow the instructions of those who are caring for me professionally but in the meantime I am going to concentrate on relaxing to the best of my ability so that both the baby and I can be as well-prepared as possible for our shared experience.

Over the past months I have grown accustomed to relaxation and its many benefits and I am going to practise that technique now – unless told otherwise by a doctor, nurse or midwife. So, beginning at my feet and working upwards, I am going to concentrate on each area of my body in turn, allowing it to become heavier and more relaxed with each breath that I take.

I know that at this time my breathing is especially important so I ensure that I breathe deeply . . . slowly . . . evenly. The more oxygen I take in with each breath, the more strength my baby will have to begin its journey into the world. For a few moments, unless told otherwise by a doctor, nurse or midwife, I am going to pay particular attention to establishing a slow breathing pattern. To make this easier, I shall count slowly and silently in my mind and with each odd number I shall breathe in, while with each even number I shall exhale. One . . . two . . . three . . . four . . . five . . . six . . . seven . . . eight . . . nine . . . ten . . . (*continue until at least number sixty*).

Now that I have established this pattern of slow breathing, it will be easy for me to continue in this way until told to do otherwise. Each time I exhale I visualize any pain or discomfort flowing out of my body and, each time I inhale, I imagine being filled with strength and energy. I know that, if I can experience these sensations, they will at the same time be transmitted to my baby.

In my mind I picture the room which is ready and waiting for the baby and I spend a few moments now visualizing it in every detail. Now, because I have grown accustomed to communicating with my child and talking to him, I am going to describe that room to him. I can choose whether to speak the words aloud or simply to communicate by thoughts.

At all times while we are waiting for the moment of birth I shall remind my baby of my love for him and how wanted he is and how cherished he will be. To make this love even more tangible, I visualize it as a soft, warm colour flowing between my mind and the baby's, filling both our beings with great caring and tenderness.

Unless told otherwise by a doctor, nurse or midwife, I shall continue in this way for as long as I wish, thus preparing us both for the exciting moment of birth.

Suggested affirmations

- Breathing brings relaxation
- Whenever I think of my baby I think of love
- Love is soft and (*insert chosen colour*).

AFTER THE BIRTH

Once a woman becomes pregnant, much time is spent thinking about the pregnancy, the labour, the room where the baby is to sleep, the possible choice of names, and all the other details which, not unnaturally, fill the mind of the mother-to-be. And yet, in many cases, comparatively little time is given to thinking about the practicalities of caring for this new, demanding person. Mother, and often father, may attend parenting classes, but changing a nappy on a life-sized doll and trying to do the same for a small, wriggling infant are very different, especially when you are terrified that you're going to do it some irreparable harm.

The first-time mother may love her new baby more than she ever thought possible but this does not mean that she won't come to dread the 2 am yell. And nothing really prepares her for the near impossibility of fitting tiny arms into tiny sleeves or the panic she experiences at some of those frantic cries – is it just a wet nappy or is her child in great pain?

This is not intended to put you off parenthood for life nor to make you think that the good does not far outweigh the bad. Some new mothers (usually those with helpful friends and family) seem to float happily through the whole experience without floundering at all. This, of course, does not help the many women who think that they are the only ones unable to cope with the demands of this new way of life. And yet, why should we think that confidence when dealing with a tiny baby should come naturally? You have to learn to be confident when riding a bicycle, driving a car or cooking a meal; and you have to learn to be confident as a mother too (which is probably why most second and subsequent children in a family seem to be so easy compared to the first one – the one you have to practise on!).

The Life Script which follows is designed to help you realize that you are not expected to be instantly adept at coping with motherhood; also to remind you that you are by no means alone in the way you feel. Use it when you are feeling low or on those days when you seem to have two left hands, each with five thumbs. If your day has been so fraught that you haven't been able to find a moment to use this script, play it to yourself just before going to bed at night. It need not take very long so you won't lose any of your precious sleep – and the benefit you feel should soon make up for those few moments you do lose. As ever, be sure to practise the relaxation technique before going on to the script itself – you need it more than ever at this time.

Confident motherhood script

As I relax at this quiet moment in my busy life, I take extra time to experience the pleasure of the release of tension from my muscles and my mind. This is *my* time – and all the more precious because there is so much less of it than there used to be.

I know that I am happy to be a mother and to have my baby safe at home with me. But I accept the fact that caring for him (her) may not be as easy as I might have previously believed. Babies do not follow a pattern; each one is different. So, no matter how many books I read or how many pieces of advice I listen to, there never has been and never will be another baby quite like mine. And this is what makes him (her) so special. He (she) has a personality and temperament all of his (her) own and, as the days go by and we grow closer and more used to each other, I will come to understand and love that personality more and more.

I accept that I may feel less than confident when dealing with my baby but, as with any other skill, I know that my confidence will grow day by day. The most important thing of all is to love him (her) as, however tiny and unable to communicate, he (she) will still be very aware of the emotions surrounding him (her). The greatest gift I can give him (her) at the moment is to surround him (her) with love; that is far more important than being seen to cope perfectly with the practical aspects of looking after him (her).

Babies grow so quickly that it is vital to make the most of every stage of their development. Even those things which may seem so difficult – the waking in the night and the endless piles of washing – will pass before too long. Every other baby eventually sleeps through the night so I know that mine will too. For the moment I shall try to adjust my own sleep pattern where possible, perhaps having a rest when he (she) sleeps during the day. I recognize that this is important, that I am a person with needs of my own and that all I am doing is temporarily readjusting my personal timetable to fit in with the demands of this tiny new member of the family.

Just as my baby was aware of surrounding atmosphere and emotion when still inside my womb, I realize that these can still have a great influence on him (her) now. Because of this, I shall do my best to be as relaxed as possible, not only when handling him (her) but at all times. So now, as I concentrate on breathing slowly and regularly, I shall let the sensation of peace and tranquillity flow over me for as long as I wish.

Although this script has been written from the point of view of the mother, because, in most families, she is still the one who will play the leading role in the baby's earliest days, there is of course no reason why it cannot be adapted for equally satisfactory use by the father.

Suggested affirmations

- Any skill develops with practice
- My baby is important – and I am important too
- The greatest thing is love.

PARENT/BABY LINKING

You were given a script earlier to assist mother/baby linking before the child was born, at a time when even the most caring father-to-be cannot play as significant a role in the baby's emotional evolvement. The script which follows is designed to continue and develop the process of linking but is suitable for use by both father and mother – either separately or, perhaps even more advantageously, together.

Because, while using this script, you are going to have close contact with your baby, by holding him and stroking him, it is obviously wise to choose a time when he is quiet and peaceful rather than trying to fit it in when you know he is growing hungry! You are also likely to find that the combination of touch, thought, words and music will soothe him at a time when he is fretful.

The ideal scenario would be one in which one parent sits cradling the baby in their arms while the other sits very close, touching the child in some way (resting a hand lightly on him or stroking him gently). Have the same music playing in the background that you used when practising mother/baby linking during the course of the pregnancy.

Parent/baby linking script

As I sit here, relaxed and comfortable, holding my baby in my arms, listening to the beautiful music we have both come to know so well, I am aware of a sensation of peace and love filling my being and binding me ever closer to the child I am holding.

I want you to know, (baby's name), that you are very special and very precious and that I am doing my best to surround you with the love I feel.

I visualize that love as a beautiful coloured light flowing between us. As my hands touch you and stroke you, I imagine that light being created in my heart, filling my mind and body and flowing from my fingertips into your body, bringing with it a sense of peace and of strength.

At the same time as this unspoken communion takes place, I visualize an aura of pure white light surrounding you and protecting you. As the music continues, this white light becomes more powerful and easier to imagine and I know that you will realize that I am sending you strength and love.

This feeling of mutual love and peace is growing so strong that, whenever I pick you up, touch your skin or hold you close, we will both be aware of it. I know that this will give you a sense of security and of your own value – which, in turn, will help you to grow up to be confident and with a strong self-image, enabling you to overcome many of life's difficulties and develop into an aware adult with a loving, caring nature.

By using this script, not only will you enjoy many moments of shared peace and love with your child, you will also be helping him to develop into an adult with a strong sense of self-esteem and confidence, thus avoiding so many of the fears and anxieties which surround any person who has not felt himself so cherished as a child.

Suggested affirmations

- Peace and love flow between us
- The white light of protection surrounds my child.

POST-NATAL DEPRESSION

This is not a topic for which a script is provided as, if you suffer from post-natal depression, you should really seek outside help. You may choose to turn to traditional or complementary medicine – or, indeed, a combination of the two. However, there are some ways in which you can help yourself.

When a woman is under stress, the amount of adrenalin she produces increases while the amount of female hormones being produced decreases. Practising a deep relaxation technique, such as the one given in the very first script in this book (particularly if done in conjunction with the music you listened to during the mother/baby linking process), decreases the amount of stress in the body. This in turn reduces the adrenalin and allows more oestrogen and progesterone to be produced.

So, although relaxation cannot be said to provide the complete answer to post-natal depression, it can certainly help to regulate the hormone production. In addition, you will have the sense of satisfaction which accompanies the knowledge that you are doing what you can to help yourself to recover fully and completely.

8

Loving Yourself

At first glance, 'Loving Yourself' might seem a strange title for a chapter. After all, doesn't loving yourself sound somewhat akin to pride and vanity? But that is not what I mean at all. In this context, loving yourself means valuing yourself as a person and appreciating your own worth. You would think, wouldn't you, that this would be the most natural thing in the world – and yet it is not. In all the years people have been consulting me at my practice, the greatest problem encountered has been that of a poor self-image. And in all the years I have been conducting seminars for companies and for individuals, those which have repeatedly been the most popular are courses in Assertiveness, Self-Awareness or Improving Self-Esteem. There are a lot of people in this world who consider themselves less talented, less worthy and less lovable than those around them.

DEALING WITH THE PAST

Feelings of low self-esteem are not created out of thin air. People are not born thinking that they are inferior; this is a state of mind forced upon them by people, events or circumstances they encounter during the early, formative years of their lives. Sometimes the poor self-image arises due to an unfortunate set of circumstances which they and those closest to them could not avoid, such as illness, death or enforced absence from home of one of their parents or situations of unrest (war, strikes, racism) around them. Sometimes the circumstances were not intended to do harm but were wrong for the child, such as over-demanding or over-protective parents, being sent to boarding school when this did not suit their personality or breaking up of the immediate family by divorce or separation. And sometimes there was actual malice involved, and the child was a victim of abuse – whether this was mental, physical, emotional or sexual.

Because a child, in his early years, has his judgements and opinions formed predominantly by the adults around him, whether they are parents, guardians, teachers or any others who stand in positions of authority, if one or more of those people should treat him badly, he will not be able to stop and work out that it is the adult who is wrong. No, in his young mind adults are always right; therefore he himself is the only person who can be wrong.

Once this view is firmly fixed in the child's mind, attitudes and circumstances are likely to reinforce it. No child is going to suffer emotional harm because he is told off or even shouted at on the odd occasion. It is the repetition of the abuse, whatever form it may take, which causes the problems. And someone who is capable of abusing a child's rights on one occasion is not going to stop there; it is likely to be an ongoing process.

One of my patients, not long divorced from an arrogant, demanding husband, said to me, 'I know that I am not stupid, but when you have been told that you *are* every day for fourteen years you come to believe it.' If an intelligent adult woman could have her opinion of herself squashed in this way, how much more vulnerable is the small child who has never known any other treatment.

If you feel that your self-esteem is lower than it should be, then the Life Scripts in this chapter are for you. It doesn't matter whether the damage was done deliberately and maliciously or whether it was as the result of an unfortunate set of circumstances. It doesn't even matter if you don't really know how the situation arose; because your subconscious mind understands the reasons perfectly well (even if you have not yet been able to acknowledge them) and because the Life Scripts work on your subconscious as well as your conscious mind, there is one designed specially to help you. Having said that, however, if you do find yourself in the position of being unaware how this loss of self-esteem came about, you would do well to make some attempt to solve the riddle – if only to prevent a recurrence at some future time.

There is one very important point to remember: it is not possible to change someone else (although, of course, they can change if they wish to) but *it is always possible to make changes in yourself*. A good starting-point is to realize and accept that something, or even many things, must have happened in your life to destroy the confidence you were entitled to feel. You may know what that 'something' is or you may not. You may even be afraid of trying to find out what it was in case the memories are painful – although, of course, they are already etched on your subconscious. For the purposes of the first script, however, you do not have to look back at any specific person or event. It is perfectly effective without that process being necessary.

This Life Script should, as always, follow on from the original relaxation technique you have been practising.

Dealing with the past script – 1

I am perfectly relaxed and aware of the sound of my own gentle breathing. I am also happy because I know that I am about to free myself from the bonds of the past and this will enable me to go forward and live my life in the way I would prefer.

As my body grows heavier and heavier with relaxation, I visualize myself standing at one end of a long corridor. It is a light, bright, pleasant corridor and I am quite content to be there. At the far end of this corridor, some distance away from me, I can see a glass door which leads to the outside. I cannot see clearly through this glass door, partly because of the distance and partly because it is made of the type of reeded glass which distorts images. But I am aware that, on the other side of that door, the sun is shining.

All along the corridor, to the right and to the left, are other doors which presumably lead to rooms. Each door is very slightly open, although not sufficiently for me to be able to see into the rooms themselves. I know that each of those rooms contains something – some person, event or occasion – from my past which has contributed to my present poor self-image. I do not know what is in each room and I never need to know. It is enough to know that something relevant is there.

In a few moments I am going to walk along that corridor and, as I come to each door on the right and on the left, I shall pause, grasp the knob or handle and gently but firmly pull the door closed. When I have closed all the doors, I shall stand in front of that reeded glass door at the far end.

(Now, working at whatever speed feels comfortable to you, imagine walking along that corridor, closing each door as you come to it.)

What I have just done, by closing all those doors, is not to pretend that the past did not exist and did not have an effect upon me but to put it where it belongs – firmly in the past. I am not trying to forget nor to convince myself that it was other than it really was. What I am doing is demonstrating that it no longer needs to affect me in the present or the future.

Now I come to the final door – the one made of glass. Although it is still closed, I can feel the sunshine coming through. Now I open the door and pass through into that sunshine and I find myself in a beautiful garden. I realize that each person has a different idea of what makes a garden beautiful and so I spend a few moments creating my own ideal. It can be neat and formal or a wilder and more

natural place; it can be one that I already know
or I can invent it. I can put into that garden all
those things I would most like to see there – perhaps
water, a greenhouse or a dovecote. And just as it
is possible to make changes in a real garden, so I
can change anything in this imagined garden any
time I wish.

There is no one in the garden but me and this
gives me a sense of peace and tranquillity. It is
my special garden; no one else has ever been there
and no one else will ever go there – although I may
choose to visualize pets or other animals and there
can certainly be birds, bees and butterflies. It is a
glorious day, warm and sunny with a soft breeze, and
I shall spend as long as I wish in this garden before
taking a few deep breaths and opening my eyes.

For this script to be effective, it should initially be used
daily. You may not notice an immediate difference in your
feelings about yourself; indeed, some people find it takes
a week or two before they are aware of any changes at all.
But, when you consider that you may be attempting to
undo the harmful effects of years, a few weeks is a short
time to wait.

Once you find that you are experiencing different
feelings about yourself, you can reduce your use of
the script to about two or three times a week. You
can always increase the number of times you use it if
you find yourself experiencing a difficult time in your
life or if you feel yourself slipping back into old ways
of thought.

Suggested affirmations

- The past belongs in the past
- I can put the past in its proper place
- There is sunshine ahead.

Shrinking images

Sometimes an otherwise happy childhood will have been marred by a single event or series of events which has left an indelible imprint on your mind. Some of those mentioned to me by my patients include:

- being involved in a car crash (even though not badly hurt)
- being evacuated during the war
- being alone in a hospital isolation ward, unable to have contact with parents
- seeing an adult have an accident
- being caught, miles from home, in a thunderstorm.

None of these events was the result of deliberate unkindness and, to a large extent, they could not have been avoided. But they were so frightening to the small child that they continued to have an effect on the adult lives for years afterwards. In fact, at the time I saw her, the 'little girl' who had suffered from an infectious disease at the age of three and been put in an isolation ward was fifty-three years old. Adult logic told her that the treatment she had received was necessary, and she had not been unkindly treated in the hospital. But imagine the horror of the situation to a three-year-old of being ill and being suddenly removed from your parents and put all by yourself in a large empty room to be poked and prodded by a group of strangers. The only time she saw her mother and father was through a large glass window at one end of the ward and she could not understand why they could not come and be with her or why she could not go home with them. This patient knew, because she had been told, that the experience had lasted about two months, but the effect on her had lasted over half a century.

Do you know of a particular period in an otherwise happy childhood which might have had some lasting effect upon you and the way you feel about yourself? If so, the Life Script which follows should help you. For the purposes of the script, I am going to use the example of the little girl alone in the isolation ward but naturally you will change the words to fit your own situation.

Dealing with the past script – 2

I am feeling very relaxed and comfortable and I know that I am about to come to terms with something in my past which has affected me for so long.

I realize that, apart from the usual trivial ups and downs which are part of every life, my childhood was basically a happy and a loving one and that the event which occurred could not really have been avoided. By dealing with this event now, I shall be able to put it in perspective once and for all and it will no longer be able to affect my life and my feelings about myself.

As I relax, breathing slowly and evenly, I imagine that scene from my childhood as if it were a huge framed picture. I see myself, tiny and pale, lying in the only occupied bed in what seemed to me at the time to be a huge, unfriendly room. At the far end of the room is a large glass window and through it I can make out the anxious faces of my mother and father. I know that the little girl in the bed cannot understand why they don't come in and cuddle her or take her home. My mother is crying and trying to smile at me at the same time; my father looks very worried.

It is important that I see this as a very large picture with as much detail as possible and in full colour. The frame can be of any design and hue but it is strong and heavy and holds the picture firmly.

Now I take a few deep breaths and in my mind I reduce that picture in size. The frame stays the same size – only the picture grows smaller and, as it does, a white border appears around it. Not only is the picture smaller but the colour is now less vibrant.

A few more breaths and the white border widens as the picture becomes smaller still and the colour paler.

It is impossible now to make out the expressions on the faces of myself and my parents.

I shall continue in this way for as long as it takes to make that picture no more than a tiny colourless snapshot set in a huge, heavy frame – a snapshot so small that it is impossible to see what is depicted there.

Once the picture has become this minute snapshot, it is of no significance and the events which led to it can have no further effect upon my life. Knowing this, I allow a feeling of peace and tranquillity to fill my being. I am free.

As with the previous script, you will probably need to use this one several times for it to have optimum effect. The difference is that, once you have laid this particular ghost to rest, you will have done so permanently and so are unlikely ever to need to use it again.

Suggested affirmations

- The images are growing smaller and detail is fading
- The event is no more than a tiny, colourless snapshot
- I am free.

UNDERSTANDING PEOPLE

We have already seen how your own view of yourself and your worth has been influenced greatly by the words, deeds and attitudes of other people. We have looked at how, because you were young and vulnerable, you automatically (whether consciously or subconsciously) assumed that these other people were right. It is time now to look carefully at the past, weigh up what happened and, if necessary, adjust your attitudes to the people concerned.

This may be more difficult than you imagine, especially if the people concerned were your parents. Our up-bringing makes it uncomfortable for us to criticize our parents or to accept the fact that they were not very good at the job or even that we do not like them.

But this is not a chapter about condemnation or hatred. There is no point replacing one negative emotion with another. This is about seeing those influential people from your past in a true light. It is possible to respect someone who did what he or she considered to be the best for you, even if that best turned out to be wrong. It is possible still to feel love for someone even though he turns out to have feet of clay – after all, genuine love rises above imperfections. However, it is also permissible to find that you do not have feelings of love, respect or even liking for someone who has deliberately set out to harm you. And sometimes the very knowledge that such a thing is allowed can bring its own great sense of relief.

Most of the psychological harm done to young children is done by people who have been emotionally crippled by their own upbringing. This does not excuse their behaviour but may go some way to help you to understand it. It is an accepted fact that, in many cases, the 'abused' – whether physically, mentally or emotionally – goes on to become the 'abuser'. But you are in a very privileged position. You are the one who can put a stop to this unhappy chain. Because you know the hurt you received and the long-term effect it has had upon you, you can make sure that, not only will you work at re-building your own self-esteem, but you will take great care not to allow anyone else to suffer because of your attitude.

There are two Life Scripts in this section. The first is designed to help you come to terms with the fact that the person (or people) who contributed to your present feelings about yourself did so either because of the mistaken impression that he was doing the best for you or because he did not have your awareness and was therefore unable to break a pattern created by previous generations.

The second script, which will be explained in more

detail later, will help you to feel and then release any natural anger which arises because of past treatment.

People who have affected me script – 1

I am feeling physically and mentally relaxed as I prepare to take a great step in my own awareness and evolvement.

I have already spent some time contemplating what in my past has led to the fact that my self-esteem is lower than I would like. I have come to the conclusion that one of the reasons was the attitude and behaviour of (*insert name*) when I was younger.

Because I was at a vulnerable and impressionable age when the negative attitude first manifested itself, I accepted it unquestioningly and was not able to consider it logically, bearing in mind (*name*)'s own personality and background.

Now I am capable of contemplating the whole situation from an adult and more aware position. I realize that (*name*)'s upbringing and the way he (she) was treated when young led to the attitude he (she) showed to me. This does not excuse it or make it right, but it does help me to understand that the fault lay in (*name*) and not, as I used to think, necessarily in me.

This realization alters the whole basis on which I have formed my opinion of myself. If I was led to believe, over a period of time, that I was a less than worthy individual, I can see how I have grown to doubt myself and my own abilities. Of course, like every other person, I have negative points as well as positive ones but I now accept that there is nothing inherently wrong with me. I can therefore work towards appreciating and enhancing my positive aspects and changing the negative ones to fit in with my new level of self-esteem.

The understanding I have reached has another

great significance. Because I now realize how easy it is for one negative person to have a negative effect upon others around him, particularly upon young children, I am in a position to break the pattern and ensure that I do not continue affecting others in the way that I have been affected.

By using this script I have chosen to put aside the heavy burden I have been carrying around for so long. I shall spend the next few moments breathing deeply, experiencing the sense of release and freedom.

Suggested affirmations

- I understand the reasons for (*name*)'s behaviour
- No one has the power to make me feel unworthy except myself
- I shall never be responsible for destroying anyone else's self-esteem.

Anger

However much we may try to understand what has caused other people to behave as they did, there are some deeds for which there is no excuse. However much someone may have suffered at the hands of others, there is never any justification for inflicting deliberate abuse upon others, particularly the young and vulnerable. This abuse may take many forms; among my patients I have had some who were physically beaten, some who were tormented by being thrown out of the house, shut in cupboards, etc. and others who were the victims of sexual abuse by those people they should have been able to trust the most.

It is interesting to note that the one thing all these victims find difficulty in experiencing is anger, even though the abuse may have taken place many years ago.

The child who is being abused does not feel anger. He

will probably feel fear and he will almost certainly feel guilt, either because he knows what is going on is wrong and thinks that therefore he must deserve it or because the adult perpetrating the abuse tells him that he must say nothing to anyone because he will be considered a liar. The sense of isolation experienced by such children is tremendous; they feel that they have nowhere to run to and no one in whom they can confide.

And these are not isolated instances. One only has to study the figures relating to the calls received by Childline to know that we are talking about *thousands* of cases each year.

If you have been the victim of serious abuse, however long ago it may have taken place, then I urge you to seek outside help. You may decide to confide in a friend or relative you can trust or you may wish to consult a professional who will be able to help you come to terms with what happened but one thing is certain – to be really free of what occurred in the past, you need to be able to talk about it.

You also need to experience anger at your former abuser – not in the sense of vengeance or viciousness which would reduce you to their level but in a way which releases the tension and self-dislike which may have grown up within you. The script which follows is designed to help you feel – and then let go of – that anger. As ever, be sure that you are as relaxed as possible before commencing.

People who have affected me script – 2

I am feeling very relaxed and very safe as I prepare to look at my emotions relating to past situations. I know that I am about to go through a cleansing process which will nullify any power over me that the past and the perpetrator of harm might have.

Even though my eyes are closed and will remain so, I imagine that I am sitting in the auditorium of a cinema waiting to watch a film. This is a private showing so I know that I am alone in the cinema but this feels right and I am quite comfortable. At the moment the curtains are closed and there is a light on the screen but no picture.

The curtains open and I can see on the screen a large, still black and white photograph of an event from my past – one which I know has led to my current feelings of insecurity. Because I am now adult and I am looking at a picture of a young child, I am capable of feeling detached from this photograph, as though it is of someone else.

When I am ready, this still, black and white photograph will become a moving picture in full colour and I can watch the events unfold on the screen as they once did in real life – but at no time will I experience any pain or distress because I am observing it in a detached way. Nothing is happening to me as I sit here in my cinema seat. The characters depicted on the screen no longer exist as they appear there so I am not observing harm being done to anyone else. What I am doing is seeing clearly the facts of the situation – and seeing them through the eyes of the adult I now am rather than the child I once was.

As I watch the scene filling the screen, I am fully aware that the child is the victim and is in no way to blame for what is happening – even though someone else might be telling him (her) that this is the case. As this becomes apparent, I feel a great sense of anger welling up inside me at the injustice and the victimization of the child. I visualize this anger as the flames of a fire building up within me. It continues to build until the film I have been watching comes to an end.

Now I get up from my seat, walk to the exit and out into the open air. I take a deep breath and then exhale, blowing the accumulated fire out of my body and into the atmosphere where it disperses and vanishes for ever. I feel a great sense of lightness and freedom.

> Once again I concentrate on relaxing as deeply
> as possible, breathing slowly and evenly, having
> released myself from feelings of guilt, anger or
> despair.

If you are trying to come to terms with a single incident of
abuse in your past, you may only need to use this script a
few times. However, if you have many experiences in the
past which need to be dealt with, adapt the script to cover
each situation, spending sufficient time on each one to
deal with it thoroughly before progressing to the next.

Once you have released the anger, you have a choice
to make. You could decide to hate or wish harm to the
person who made you suffer – but what a waste of your
energy that would be. Surely it would be better to use that
energy positively to create a brighter and happier future
for yourself. Or you can decide that they are simply not
worth bothering about and let them go. This may mean
cutting them out of your life altogether or, if you choose
not to do that, letting them become so unimportant to you
that they are not worth wasting your thoughts on.

Suggested affirmations

- I release the anger from within me
- (*Name*) is no longer significant in my life
- I choose to use my energy positively.

SELF-ESTEEM

I wonder why we are all so much better at listing our
bad points than our good ones. Perhaps it seems vain or
immodest to contemplate positive things about ourselves.
And yet, if we are not honest with ourselves, about

the good and the bad, how can we ever set about making changes?

Over the next few days, make a list of all those things about yourself which you believe to be worthwhile or likeable and, at the same time, make another list of all the negative aspects of your personality. Be honest; no one is going to see this list except you so there is no need to be artificially vain or modest. I have deliberately suggested that you make your list over the course of a few days because, if you were to do it all in one session, the length of each column would be determined to a great extent by your mood on that day.

To guide you, below is an actual list compiled by one of my patients (I'll call him Paul) which he has given me permission to reproduce here:

Positive points	Negative points
Kind	Weak
Sensitive	Shy
Loyal	No confidence
Honest and trustworthy	Bad with people
Good sense of humour	Poor conversationalist
Loving to family	Under-achiever
	Too cautious
	Indecisive

Using these lists as a basis, I am going to show you how I worked with Paul by means of Life Scripts. Naturally you will adapt the words to suit the aspects of yourself you have mentioned in your own lists.

First I asked Paul to study the list of positive traits he had written. I suggested that, if he were to find someone else with all those characteristics, he would probably think he must be quite a nice fellow. Paul agreed, but then went on to say that on a bad day he found it difficult even to believe those positive things about himself – although, needless to say, he never experienced any difficulty in accepting the negative aspects! It may be that you feel as he did.

The first Life Script, therefore, is designed to help you fix those positive thoughts about yourself in your subconscious mind.

Self-esteem script – 1

I have just spent some time relaxing and ridding my body of all accumulated stress and tension. Now I am ready to proceed to the important process of improving my self-esteem.

In my relaxed state I am going to recall, one by one, all my positive traits which I put on the list. I know that they are all good aspects of my personality and that they themselves do not disappear, only, on occasions, my belief in them.

As I contemplate each characteristic in turn, I am going to 'fix' it in my subconscious mind. To achieve this, all I need do is link some simple physical action with the thought of the personality aspect. The action I am going to use is the pressing together of the thumb and first finger of my right hand and the thumb and first finger of my left hand. In readiness for this process, I place my hands in the appropriate position, finger and thumb of each hand just touching.

Now I shall take each characteristic in turn and as I think of the word I shall gently but firmly exert the pressure between thumbs and first fingers of each hand.

The first characteristic on my list is 'Kind'. As I think of the word, I exert that gentle pressure and thereby fix the belief in my own kindness in my subconscious mind.

Now I move on to the second trait, 'Sensitive', and once again I fix it in the same way.

The third word is 'Loyal'. As I think of my loyal nature, I fix the thought.

Next comes 'Honest and Trustworthy' – and I fix it.

Then follows 'Good sense of humour' and this too is fixed in the same way.

Finally I think of the fact that I am 'Loving to my

family' and I fix the thought by exerting that same gentle pressure between my thumbs and forefingers.

Now that I have fixed these beliefs about myself in my subconsious mind, I can use the same gentle physical movement to reinforce my self-esteem whenever I feel the need to do so.

Whenever I find myself lacking in a positive attitude about myself or at times when my confidence is at a low ebb, all I have to do is exert that pressure between the thumb and first finger of each hand and my subconscious will work to enhance and improve my self-image. It is such a simple movement that no one else will be able to tell what I am doing. I can do it in any place and at any time. I do not have to think consciously of the words I wrote on my list – my subconscious mind will do that for me and I will automatically feel more confident.

And that is what will happen. No matter where you find yourself – meeting a group of strangers, in an interview situation, starting a new job – that small, simple physical action will stimulate your subconscious thoughts and your self-esteem will be enhanced. (Of course, the characteristics you decide to fix may not be the same as those on Paul's list – so simply substitute your own for those in the script.)

Suggested affirmations

- My feelings about myself are governed by my subconscious mind
- I can fix good feelings
- Whenever I repeat the fixing technique my self-esteem will increase.

Returning to Paul and his lists. Having dealt with the positive aspects, we then went on to look at what he considered to be his negative traits. Although there were

eight items on his list, several of them were simply
different ways of saying almost the same thing; 'shy',
'bad with people', 'poor conversationalist' – these were
all different ways of looking at the same problem. And, as
on so many lists compiled by people with low self-esteem,
'no confidence' was there too.

In the many years I have been working as a hypnotherapist and counsellor, 'lack of confidence' is probably
the phrase which has been expressed most often by those
consulting me. And yet, to help someone overcome this
problem, it is necessary to go into far more detail. In what
area is the person lacking in confidence? It is quite rare
for someone to have no confidence at all in any area of
their life. The man or woman who finds it difficult to form
relationships may be quietly confident about their ability
to do their job well. Equally, the person who is relatively
sure of himself in the home environment may have feelings
of inadequacy at work.

I asked Paul to define what 'lack of confidence' meant
to him and he told me that firstly he felt unable to talk easily
to other people as he believed he had nothing worthwhile
to say, and secondly he was afraid to stretch himself by
trying something new or taking on added responsibility
in case he failed and made a fool of himself. These points
were really covered already in the list he had compiled as
'bad conversationalist' and 'under-achiever'.

Bearing that in mind, I asked Paul to study his negative
list and decide which aspect of his personality he would
most like to change. After some consideration he selected
'shy' as he felt that overcoming this would open doors and
lead to improvement in many of the other areas.

Now he had to define his shyness. Was he shy with
people he already knew? Did he find it equally difficult
to be in large groups of people as small ones? Was he able
to cover up his shyness so that others were unaware of
how he was feeling inside?

Paul said that he had no problem at all with members of
the family or people he already knew, whether socially or
at work. The internal turmoil he felt was the same whether
the group of new people was large or small, although he

felt he could 'hide' more effectively in a large group as it was probable that no one would realize that he was not contributing to the conversation. He felt that people meeting him for the first time often considered him to be 'stuck-up' or 'standoffish', mistaking his shyness for an aloof attitude.

So we decided to use the next Life Script to improve his attitude and behaviour when meeting a group of people for the first time. You will be able to adapt the script to deal with whatever turns out to be number one on your own list of negative traits.

Self-esteem script – 2

I am comfortably relaxed and my breathing is regular and even. I am going to concentrate on these feelings for a few moments.

Now I am ready to deal with the difficulty I have encountered until now when meeting a group of people who are unknown to me. To do this I am going to use the most powerful tools in my possession – my own imagination and my powers of visualization.

First, while still breathing slowly and calmly, I create a situation in my mind. I am about to enter a room in which there are many people, most of whom I do not know at all and a few with whom I am casually acquainted. I visualize myself outside the door of that room, just about to go in. Before I do, I take a couple of deep breaths and concentrate on releasing the tension from my neck and jaw. Then I place my hand on the doorknob and enter the room.

I wait for a few moments just inside the door and I look around the room. People are standing around in small groups, talking quietly. Because I realize that I am not alone in feeling shy, I look about me and I see a woman in whom I recognize the signs of shyness. She is standing close to a group but is not speaking and does not really look as though she is involved in any way. Sympathizing with her, I take a deep breath and, still feeling quite relaxed, I walk over to her. When I reach her I smile and ask her something quite trivial about the weather, the time of year or whether she had to make a long journey. She seems pleased that someone has chosen to speak to her and she answers my question.

We continue speaking for a while and I am happy that I have been able to put her at her ease. This increases both my relaxation and my confidence in the current situation. Gradually we extend our little group from two to three people and then to four and we find that we are all able to talk naturally and easily together.

I know that by rehearsing this situation in my mind several times over a comparatively short space of time – always concentrating on the sensation of being relaxed – I shall be able to convince my subconscious that I can cope satisfactorily with it. When the time comes to put my new-found skill into practice, it will be far easier than I could ever have imagined and it will be something which will never again cause me any anxiety.

Once again I concentrate on relaxing and breathing evenly and I allow myself to feel the joy that comes with knowing I have taken control of my life and overcome something which was formerly a problem to me.

For a visualization like this to work, you need to rehearse it several times – ideally on a daily basis for at least three weeks. What you are doing, of course, is programming your subconscious mind to believe that you are someone who can cope perfectly well with the situation you have imagined. And, if your subconscious mind is convinced, you *will* cope with it from now onwards.

You will notice that I have suggested you begin by asking a question. If you do that, the person you have spoken to will have to answer whereas, if very shy, they could simply smile and nod in response to a statement. And you don't have to rely on thinking of something to say when you get there. Why not have a couple of simple questions in your mind before you even enter the room?

Once you have dealt with the first problem on your list of negative traits, you can go on to deal with the others one by one. Please don't try to work on them all at once – your subconscious will become confused and you will achieve nothing.

Suggested affirmations

- If I can visualize it, I can do it
- My imagination is my greatest tool
- I am dealing with my problems one by one.

It is essential to accept that, whatever happened in the past to create in you a low self-esteem, *you and only you* have the ability to make the desired changes. No one else has the power now to make you feel inferior – only you. You can't change the past – you didn't choose it; but you can choose and change your future. The next chapter will help you to set some goals for that future and then work towards achieving them.

9

Looking to the Future

If you get into the habit of using Life Scripts as a means of harnessing the power of your subconscious mind, you can become one of those fortunate people who takes control of their own life and works towards making their future as they would truly wish it to be.

But, of course, if you are to work towards creating that ideal future, you first of all need to know precisely what it is that you want. Setting goals is extremely important – and these goals should be as detailed as possible. Naturally we all want to be 'happy', but what exactly would make *you* happy? We would all like to be 'successful', but what does that word convey to *you*? 'Success' might mean something very different to the student about to sit for final exams and the lonely person yearning for a friend.

It is harder than you think to decide what you would really like to achieve in the future. In fact, it is probably easier to list those things you do *not* want. You may recall the old tale of the good fairy offering the poor man three wishes which the unfortunate fellow wasted and so was left no better than before. You have one great advantage over the man in the fairy story; you have an unlimited number of wishes at your command. So, if you happen to change your mind or if your circumstances alter in such a way that a new wish comes to the fore, all you have to do is create another Life Script.

So the first thing to do is to take some time to think about the direction in which you would like your life to go. Simply doing that (thinking about it) puts you ahead of most of the population. In his book, *Success is an Inside Job*, Frank G. Thompson says:

'It has been said that only five per cent of the people think. Another fifteen per cent think they think – and the rest would rather die than think!'

If you have a wish, a dream or an ambition and you don't act upon it, you have no one but yourself to blame if you find yourself approaching the end of your life saying, 'If only . . .' And luck really plays quite a small part in the process. It is only the negative people who complain that others seem to get all the luck. Perhaps there is an element of being 'in the right place at the right time' – or perhaps it is merely a reinforcement of the old adage that 'positivity attracts positivity while negativity attracts negativity'. In other words, maybe those people with the dream who are determined to do all they can to make it come true exude such a sense of positivity and belief in themselves that those who are in a position to help them are naturally drawn to them.

Suppose you were in a position to help someone along the road to their own dream, who would you be more likely to approach – the person with the confident and positive attitude or the one who gave the impression that he would do his best but didn't really believe that he could make it?

Life Scripts play a dual role. On the one hand they actively work on your subconscious mind, enabling you to create a belief in yourself and in what you intend to achieve. On the other, the amount of repetition involved in using them regularly keeps to the forefront of your conscious mind the fact that you are doing something practical to help yourself on the road to your ambition. This in turn enhances your sense of self-esteem and makes success even more likely.

SETTING GOALS

There are various stages to goal-setting and each one
requires a different combination of logic and instinct.
Let's take them one at a time.

Long-term goals

Long-term can mean any time in the future but for the
purpose of this exercise let's assume that it is a maximum
of somewhere between five and eight years. Any plans for
further in the future may well have to be altered slightly
as you grow and develop. In addition, if you set goals for
too far ahead, you might have to wait too long to see any
positive changes.

Bear in mind that you can deal with any or all aspects of
your life when setting your long-term goals. For example,
you might want to:

- own your own home
- have your own business
- be married.

The creation of long-term goals involves as much spontaneity as possible. So, take a clean sheet of paper, head
it 'Long-term goals' and then write down three or more
things you instinctively feel that you want to achieve. At
this stage it is important not to stop and wonder whether
you are likely to achieve them or whether you are taking
on an impossible task. Be spontaneous and be honest. No
one but you need ever see this piece of paper so make sure
you put down what you *really* want.

If you do this as you should – that is, without too much
prior thought – you may even find that one or more of
the goals you have written surprises you. Sometimes,
particularly if you have not been brought up to think
of yourself as someone who achieves their desires, you
will have spent so much time being careful or settling for
something other than the best that your true ambitions

will have been locked deep within you. That is why I ask you to complete this section fairly rapidly.

Mid-term goals

If the long-term goal caused you to look some five to eight years into the future, then the mid-term goals should be those you hope to have attained in two to four years from now.

This section calls for a little more thought. Taking each of the long-term goals in turn, ask yourself what stage you would need to have reached in two to four years if those goals are to stand a chance of becoming possible. There is no point in hoping for a happy marriage if you never go out and meet other people. And there is no possibility of running a successful business, whatever your background, if you do not have some basic business skills at your fingertips.

Because you are still looking quite some way into the future, don't be too detailed at this point.

Short-term goals

These are the things you would need to have attained in about a year from now if your mid-term goals are to be viable. (Your long-term goals have now become something to keep in the back of your mind but do not need consideration here – you are only looking ahead at this point to those mid-term ambitions.)

Completing this section takes more thought still. In fact, it is often a good idea to let it take a few days. What you are doing, in effect, is working out a plan of campaign which is going to enable you to work towards attaining what you really want in life – so it is essential to spend more time considering what to do.

In the legend there was no doubt as to whether or not the good fairy would grant the three wishes. In the same way, this is not an 'if only' section – this is an actual blueprint for what you intend to be doing during the next year. Knowing what you want in such detail is more than half the battle – and you will have your Life Scripts to help you all along the way.

Immediate goals

You know what you want in the long term; you know where you will need to be in about two or three years if you are to attain those long-term goals; you know what you are going to have to achieve in the next year or so. Now, what are you going to do next week?

Yes, I said next week. And there is something you can do, whatever your goals. It may be something as basic as finding out more information or putting your name down for a course. It may be reading a book on a topic which interests you and which could play a role in attaining those long-term goals. What it is only you can decide – but decide you must!

Once you have thought of something you can do next week, write it down. Fix it to the bathroom mirror, the refrigerator or your car dashboard – somewhere where you cannot avoid looking at it every single day. That is your commitment for the coming week. If you really hope to attain those goals, then get out there and *do it*! You will feel so good afterwards because you will know that, however simple this first task has been, you have actually taken the first step towards the goals you have chosen.

Intuitive goal-setting

You will have seen that the setting of those long-term goals involved the use of instinct or intuition and it may be that this is something you find difficult. We all began our lives as intuitive beings but, as described in the section on left and right brain, our upbringing may well have caused us temporarily to lose sight of this facility. If you feel that this applies to you and if you experienced difficulty in being sufficiently spontaneous when compiling your long-term goals, here is a Life Script which will help you. Use it (after the usual relaxation technique) at the very beginning of the goal-setting process.

Goal-setting script

I am feeling warm, relaxed and comfortable and I am going to contact my inner self in order to use my intuition to discover my true goals in life.

In my imagination I visualize myself standing at the top of a grass-covered hill. This is a lovely spot and as I look around me I can see the blue sky and soft white clouds above me and the valley deep below. It is a beautiful day and I am happy to be standing here. In my hand I have a sheet of white paper on which is written nothing but a date. That date is five years from now.

I look down and see that I am standing on a tiny footpath, just wide enough for one person, which leads around the hill and downwards. I decide to follow this path and see where it takes me. And so I begin to walk.

This is a pleasant place to be and I enjoy strolling on this downward path, looking around me at the beautiful scenery. As I walk, the path becomes slightly wider and more clearly defined.

This walk can take as long as I like but now I find my attention drawn to a cottage nestling among some trees on the lower slopes of the hill. I realize that the footpath I am now on will take me all the way down to that cottage and I feel a need to discover who lives there. Somehow I know that, whoever it is, that person will be able to help me re-kindle my intuitive abilities. I am so excited at this thought that I find myself walking more quickly in my eagerness to reach the cottage.

And here I am, standing at the gate to the cottage. I lift the latch and open the gate. The path I have been following takes me right up to the front door. As I reach the front door, it opens and I stand face to face with someone I immediately recognize to be a man (*if you are a man; or woman, if you are a woman*) of great wisdom. He smiles and, without speaking, invites me into his home.

I follow this wise man across the hallway and into a room. The room is warm and comfortable and I feel completely at ease. The walls are lined with shelves of books and there is a large comfortable chair in front of the fireplace. The wise man indicates that I should sit in this chair and I do so. It is so comfortable that it feels as though it was made just for me.

Now the wise man is holding out his hand and I realize he is asking for my piece of paper. I give it to him. He turns away and goes immediately to the bookshelves. Running his hand along one of the shelves, he selects a large volume and brings it to me where I sit. He opens the book seemingly at random and hands it to me. The left-hand page is blank but on the right-hand page is a picture of me as I shall be when I have attained one of my long-term goals. As I look at it, I realize precisely what that goal is.

I hand the book back to the wise man and, thanking him, I turn and leave the room. Crossing the hallway, I go out of the front door and along the path to the gate. I continue along the footpath which brought me to the cottage and, after walking a short distance, I turn and look back.

The gate is still open; the front door is still open; and, although I cannot see it, I know that the door to the book-filled room is still open. The wise man is standing at the door, waiting for me to return whenever I wish. I continue up to the top of the hill until I feel I could almost touch the clouds. And here I remain until I feel that I want to open my eyes.

This is an excellent way of gaining access to your sub-conscious wishes and desires and should prove effective if you are having difficulty in using your intuition when trying to decide on your long-term goals.

If you are only having difficulty in one area of goal-setting, then the script as it is given above should be sufficient. However, if you feel that you really do not know what you want in any aspect of your life, alter the script slightly so that the wise man hands you the book a number of times, each time open at a different page.

Suggested affirmations

- My subconscious mind knows what I really want
- The wise man (woman) is my inner self
- I can attain my goals.

CREATING YOUR OWN LIFE SCRIPTS

There may be various reasons why you feel the need to create your own personal Life Scripts. Perhaps, now that you have decided upon your goals, you need a script to help you at each stage. Or perhaps you have a current problem which is not covered by the Life Scripts given so far. Whatever the reason, there is a simple step-by-step technique you can follow to create the perfect script for your needs.

- Be perfectly clear in your own mind exactly what you wish to achieve. Take some time thinking about it. Ask yourself where you stand at the moment, what changes you would like to make – and whether those changes are reasonable ones. If you have a quiet and gentle personality, you may wish to become more assertive and more confident, but think twice before trying to make yourself into a vivacious centre-of-the-fun extrovert. Would such a dramatic change really make you happy? If it would, then by all means go for it but remember that it is very difficult to put on an act for any length of time and there is no point trying to become something you do not truly want.

- Write your script. Think carefully about the words you choose. This is not a script listing your hopes and aspirations. The words must indicate a confidence that you are *certain* to attain, whatever it is you are working towards. Make the script as personal as possible – inserting names, dates or images which have a special meaning to you; it will be so much more effective. And use your own style and language; don't try to copy mine or anyone else's. You are your own person and *you* are the one who will have to work from this script so write (and then speak) in the way you normally do.

- Incorporate as much visualization as possible. This is why you need to be sure of what it is that you want to achieve. The more detailed you can make your imagery, the more effective the script will be and the more likely you are to get precisely what you want.

- When you think you have completed your written script, practise reading it aloud a couple of times. Does it read naturally? Does it sound like *you*? Have you incorporated as much detail as possible? Will you feel comfortable listening to it over and over again? If not, this is the time to make alterations.

- Now you are ready to record your script on cassette. Here are a few hints which will help you to do this well: – Because each script needs to be preceded by the relaxation technique, you might like to record this first and then follow on with your new script. – Speak slowly. Much more slowly than you would have believed necessary. You have written these words with care; you want them to be heard and absorbed when you come to listen to the script. Leave pauses after any particularly important statement or image. This will allow your subconscious mind to enlarge or enhance any visualization you have described. – If your cassette recorder has a separate microphone, don't be tempted to speak down into it. You will make a much clearer recording if you hold the microphone at chin level and look straight ahead as you speak. – You may decide you would like to use some relaxing music in the background as you speak. This is more difficult to achieve than you might think so experiment a little first. Test for volume – you don't want the music to become intrusive. And be sure to select a piece you can bear to hear day after day – if you become bored with it, you will eventually give up playing the cassette altogether.

- Write your affirmations. There should be at least two or three – although, of course, you can have as many as you want. Keep them short, positive and to the point.

Once you have recorded your cassette, use it regularly. It is probably best to listen to it daily at first, reducing it to about three times a week when you find it is beginning to have an effect. When you feel you have achieved what you set out to by means of the first Life Script, it is time to go on to the next.

MAKING CHANGES

There may be any number of reasons why you will decide to change your goals, particularly the long-term ones, as you go along. This is quite acceptable and is why I suggested that the long-term goals should be more instinctive and less detailed than the others.

These changes may be brought about by external situations which are beyond your control. That is fine and should not cause you to become anxious or to think that you can no longer go in the direction you have chosen. After all, if you set out in the car one afternoon to visit Auntie Jean for tea only to discover that the road is under repair and there are diversion signs taking you away from your usual route, what do you do? You don't say, 'Oh, well, that's it,' and turn round and head for home. No, you follow those diversion signs and, even if it takes you a little longer and the route is unfamiliar, you still end up at Auntie Jean's house.

In just the same way, if you find you have to make

alterations in your route, it does not mean that you will not attain your goals in the end.

Of course the changes may not be forced upon you at all. They may simply arise because your hopes and ambitions have changed and you realize that what you wanted in the beginning is not what you want now. This does not mean that you have failed or even that you made a mistake. Nothing has been wasted and nothing has been lost. Whatever you have achieved to date, even if it appears to have no bearing on what you now perceive as your future, has all been part of an essential learning process and will have taught you a good deal about yourself.

What is a mistake if not a chance to do something in a different way? Even if all you learn is that you now know what you *don't* want, that is a great deal more than some people ever realize! Remember that a problem is just an opportunity in disguise.

So now it is up to you. Remember that anything your subconscious mind creates, you are capable of achieving. Your subconscious simply will not accept that which is impossible. Yes, the system takes planning and, yes, it takes a certain amount of dedication on your part. But, not only does it become easier and more of a habit as time goes on (you don't forget to clean your teeth, do you?), you will experience a great excitement as you start to see results. And that elation is all the greater because you know that *you* have created your own success.

Enjoy Life Scripts. Learn to make them work for you and they will help and benefit you and those you care about for the rest of your life.

Appendix

USEFUL READING

Helmstetter, S. *What to Say When You Talk to Yourself* (Thorsons, 1986)
Markham, U. *Elements of Visualisation* (Element Books, 1991)
Markham, U. *Living with Change* (Element Books, 1993)
Syer, J. and Connolly, C. *Think to Win* (Simon & Schuster, 1991)
Thompson, F. G. *Success is an Inside Job* (Diliton Publications, 1981)

ORGANIZATIONS

(When contacting any organization, please enclose a stamped addressed envelope.)

The Miscarriage Association
PO Box 24
Ossett, West Yorkshire

Foresight
The Old Vicarage
Church Lane
Godalming, Surrey
GU8 5PN

SELF-HELP CASSETTES AND SELF-AWARENESS TRAINING

The Hypnothink Foundation
PO Box 154
Cheltenham
Glos.
GL53 9EG

If you would like an individually-prepared and personalized Life Script cassette, please contact Ursula Markham at The Hypnothink Foundation, PO Box 154, Cheltenham, Glos. GL53 9EG for further information.

Index